Airport Spotting Guides

Asia & the Far East

DestinWorld
publishing

First published 2018

Destinworld Publishing Ltd
www.destinworld.com

British Library Cataloguing in Publication Data.
A catalogue record for this book is available from the British Library.

ISBN 978 1 9996470 0 1

Cover design by John Wright

Printed and bound in Great Britain by Marston Book Services Ltd, Oxfordshire

CONTENTS

INTRODUCTION

Thank you for purchasing this guide to one of the most interesting parts of the world for aviation enthusiasts. Air travel in Asia and the Far East has grown into an enormous industry, with many of the world's largest hub airports and largest, most well-regarded airlines.

China itself is an emerging region with some of the world's largest and busiest airports, and hundreds more airports planned for the future, not to mention its own manufacturing plants and airlines with fleets of hundreds of aircraft.

The region is also thriving for low-cost carriers, which makes travel between all major cities easy and affordable. Combined with cheap airport hotels (many have great views), a trip you might plan around the highlights need not break the bank.

Whilst spotting is still not understood or tolerated in some areas, others welcome it and provide facilities to make the hobby easier. In Japan, nearly all airports – big or small – provide a viewing terrace on the terminal, making it one of the world's most spotter friendly countries.

With this edition we have covered more airports than previous guides to Asia. I hope the final result will prove useful and interesting to you in planning your spotting trips, or using for on-the-go research.

Notes on Using This Guide

As always, the information provided is for use at your own risk. We do not take any responsibility for your actions when visiting the airports listed here, or using the information provided. Maps are our own interpretations, and are not meant to be used for navigation.

You should always ensure you have permission to spot aircraft from private property, and the advice we'd always stand by is that informing airport police or security officers of your intentions is a good thing. Most will be perfectly happy to allow you to continue, or to suggest a better place to stand.

Information provided in this book is always subject to going out of date; airports develop, roads and rights of way change, and perhaps most common of all, the airline operators and aircraft types being used will change. We have done everything to ensure the information provided in this book is correct at the time of publication, but must warn that it can go out of date.

Keep up with changes in the world of airports and spotting at www.airportspotting.com

SPOTTING IN ASIA: THE ESSENTIALS

Asia technically covers the entire region from the Middle East to the island nations in the western Pacific. This book covers the countries eastwards from India, including all of the Far East and its many hub airports.

Some countries, like Pakistan, Afghanistan and Kazakhstan, have been omitted as they are not places we would recommend spotting in.

Deciding where to visit in Asia really depends on the purpose of your trip. For an enthusiast who wants to discover the sights and aircraft on offer, any trip needs to be carefully planned and will likely only take in one area or a selection highlights – particularly if you have never visited the region before. In this section I want to give an overview of what those highlights might be, depending on your own particular interests.

For the general spotter interested in airliners, the most practical advice would be to focus on some of the larger hub airports where sheer numbers of aircraft will satisfy any logbook or camera lens. Each country's major airlines focus on a few hubs or bases. Among the best hub airports in Asia and the Far East for enthusiasts are Bangkok Suvarnabhumi, Beijing Capital, Hong Kong Chek Lap Kok, Jakarta Soekarno-Hatta, Kuala Lumpur, Manila, Seoul Incheon, Shanghai Pudong, Singapore and Tokyo's two airports.

Then there are the smaller, often original airports in each city which now largely provide a domestic or regional role. In many cases these are still incredibly busy places, with domestic airline fleets that you won't see elsewhere. Examples include Bangkok Don Mueang, Seoul Gimpo, Shanghai Hongqiao and Taipei Songshan. Choosing a selection of these airports on a trip will certainly keep you busy.

If older aircraft are your thing, there are some excellent museums across Asia where you can indulge in padding out your logbook with retired types. The best is at Beijing's Datangshan Museum where hundreds of aircraft await you. Others include the Tokorozawa Aviation Museum near Tokyo, the Philippine Air Force Aerospace Museum in Manila, and the Royal Thai Air Force Museum in Bangkok.

Whilst on the subject of older aircraft, braver enthusiasts often venture on organised tours to Asia's most secretive country, North Korea. Here, national airline Air Koryo still flies some classic Soviet airliners.

The best advice for someone new to visiting Asia is to take in a few of the major hubs, and arrange travel between them on low-cost airlines. If you're a veteran of the area, it's really about working out where you haven't been yet, or where the largest gaps in your logs are. China is the fastest growing country and its airlines are adding to their fleets all the time. Whereas countries like Cambodia and Laos may not be as busy, but offer something of the past which may add variety to your trip.

Whatever you choose, it's easier than ever to get to Asia, either direct on one of the many long-haul links from Europe and North America, or via one of the Middle Eastern hubs.

Remember that many countries will require a visa for your visit. You should investigate whether this is required before travel, or if it can be applied for upon arrival. Most offer a tourist visa for shorter stays, and places like China allow a 72-hour transit, which is perfect if you're stopping by for some spotting in between two other countries.

ASIA'S TOP 20 SPOTTING LOCATIONS?

Reading through this guide, you will discover many different locations. Your favourite will no doubt match the aircraft you want to see, or the parts of the country you are visiting. However, here are my suggestions of the best spotting locations on offer.

1. Tokyo Haneda Observation Decks
2. Phuket Nai Yang Beach
3. Osaka Kansai Sky View Observation Hall
4. Kuala Lumpur International Viewing Galleries
5. Beijing Capital Viewing Mound
6. Tokyo Narita Observation Decks
7. Jakarta Soekarno Hatta Airport Hotel
8. Singapore Changi Crowne Plaza Hotel
9. Bangkok Suvarnabhumi Observation Area
10. Osaka Itami Sky Park
11. Singapore Changi Viewing Malls
12. Hong Kong Sky Deck
13. Taipei Songshan Observation Deck
14. Chubu Centrai Observation Deck
15. Fukuoka Observation Decks
16. Manila Holiday Inn Express
17. Bangkok Don Mueang Observation Area
18. Jakarta Soekarno Hatta Waving Galleries
19. Guangzhou Pullman Hotel
20. Surabaya Waving Gallery

BANGLADESH

Capital: Dhaka

DHAKA

Overview

Bangladesh is a poor and crowded country which suffers from its lowland location. Nevertheless, its national airline Biman has been growing in recent years and now has a modern fleet which has replaced the ageing classic jets it once flew.

The country's main gateway at Dhaka is a place which can be part of a stop-over when heading to or from Asia, giving you an opportunity to visit to see what you can from the aircraft without staying longer.

DHAKA SHAHJALAL INTERNATIONAL

DAC | VGHS

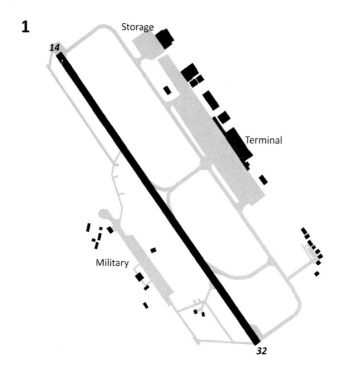

Dhaka is the home base of Biman Bangladesh Airlines and it is served by many international carriers. It has a single runway and terminal on the eastern side, with Biman's maintenance facilities to the north. A military base exists on the opposite side.

Those transiting without leaving the airport should be able to see most civil aircraft on the ground from your own aircraft. You may also see some retired types in a compound to the north.

There are also views from within the terminal.

BASE FOR:
Biman Bangladesh
Novoair
Regent Airways
US-Bangla Airlines

↓

If you venture outside, there is a café at the end of runway 14 with great views of aircraft approaching (1). It is known as the Café Runway, and can be found on Bawnia Road.

REGULAR:
Air Arabia
AirAsia
Air India
Cargolux
Cathay Dragon
Cathay Pacific Cargo
China Airlines Cargo
China Eastern
China Southern
Druk Air
Emirates
Etihad
FitsAir
Gulf Air
IndiGo
Jet Airways
Korean Air Cargo
Kuwait Airways
Malaysia Airlines
Maldivian
Malindo Air
Martinair
Pakistan International
Qatar Airways
SalamAir
Saudia
Scoot
Silk Way
Singapore Airlines
SpiceJet
SriLankan Airlines
Thai Airways
Thai Lion Air
TransGlobal Airways
Turkish Airlines

BHUTAN

Capital: Thimphu

Overview

Bhutan is a country set among the Himalayas between India and China, close to Bangladesh and Nepal. It's history and scenery draws many tourists, yet the terrain proves difficult for air operators.

The main airport gateway is at Paro, where national carriers Bhutan Airlines and Druk Air are based. There are four airports in total in Bhutan – Gelephu, Bathpalathang, Paro and Yongphulla. Only Paro has international flights.

PRINCIPAL AIRPORTS

PARO AIRPORT

PBH | VQPR

Paro International is the main gateway to Bhutan, and one of the most challenging airports in the world owing to its position in a twisting valley surrounding by mountains. Pilots need to be certified to land here, where the runway sits at over 7,000ft above sea level.

Airliner movements are almost entirely made up of Bhutan Airlines Airbus A319s, and Druk Air A319, A320 and ATR 42 aircraft. There are also helicopter and local operators.

Those wanting to watch movements can do so from the road running parallel to the runway on its eastern side. All aircraft on the ground can be seen from the various vantage points here, and at either end of the runway positions on slightly higher ground can be found to watch aircraft landing or departing.

BASE FOR:
Bhutan Airlines
Druk Air

BRUNEI

Capital: Bandar Seri Begawan

BANDAR SERI BEGAWAN

Overview

The tiny nation of Brunei, on the island of Borneo and surrounded by Malaysia, is home to a single airport at the capital, Bandar Seri Begawan.

This airport is the base for Royal Brunei Airlines and also the country's air force.

PRINCIPAL AIRPORTS

BANDAR SERI BEGAWAN

BWN | WBSB

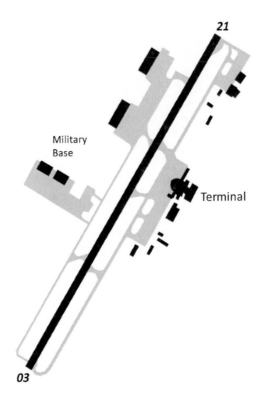

The only airport in Brunei, and home to the national carrier. Bandar Seri Begawan is a mixed civil-military airfield with a single runway, 03/21. The modest passenger terminal is on the eastern side, with the Royal Brunei Air Force base occupying a site on the western side.

There are also cargo facilities and a maintenance base for Royal Brunei Airlines.

BASE FOR:
Royal Brunei

REGULAR:
AirAsia
Cebu Pacific
Lucky Air
Malaysia Airlines
SilkAir
Singapore Airlines

Movements are dominated by the national carrier. Others include a mix of low-cost and full-service carriers from around Asia, with many passengers in transit through the airport.

The airport is not busy by the standards of other Asian hubs. Those passing through have good views of the runway from the departure gates.

Spotting locations around the airport are hard to come by, and it is not advised to explore too much, particularly near the air base.

CAMBODIA

Capital: Phnom Penh

Overview

Air travel in Cambodia is focussed on the capital, Phnom Penh, which handles the majority of the international flights coming to the country, and its significant amount of tourism. Siem Reap and Sihanoukville are also moderately busy airports. None are on a par with the airports of neighbouring countries like China, Thailand and Vietnam, but make for an interesting diversion with some of the local carriers and their aircraft.

Spotting is not particularly understood in Cambodia, and many of the airports double up as military bases, so be cautious with the use of cameras and binoculars.

PHNOM PENH INTERNATIONAL

PNH | VDPP

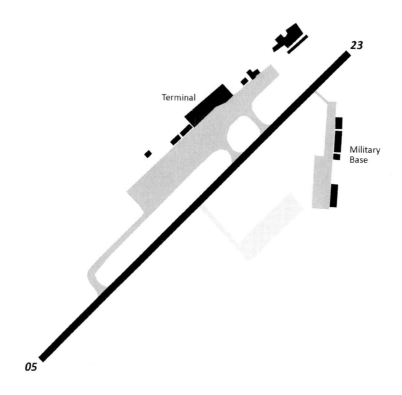

Cambodia's capital airport is a base for the country's main carriers, with various other international airlines providing links across Asia and the Middle East. The airport is not particularly big, with one runway and two terminals – domestic and international. It is anticipated, however, that a new, much larger airport will be built to the south of the city.

BASE FOR:
Bassaka Air
Cambodia Angkor Air
JC International
Lanmei Airlines

↓

Phnom Penh shares its runway with the Pochentong Air Base, which occupies a site on the eastern side of the field. Various Antonov transport aircraft, plus fast jets and helicopters, operate from here, and you may see some stored aircraft alongside the base.

It is not advisable to try and visit the air base without permission, and spotting around the airport perimeter can be difficult without attracting unwanted attention.

Therefore, the best place to watch aircraft is inside the departure lounge for those taking a flight. The windows are amble to see aircraft parked at the gates and on the runway beyond.

REGULAR:
AirAsia
AirBridgeCargo
All Nippon Airways
Asiana
Bangkok Airways
Beijing Capital
Cathay Dragon
China Airlines
China Eastern
China Express
China Southern
Emirates
EVA Air
Hainan Airlines
Hong Kong Airlines
Jetstar Asia
Korean Air
Malaysia Airlines
Malindo Air
Qatar Airways
SF Airlines
Shandong Airlines
Shenzhen Airlines
SilkAir
Spring Airlines
Thai AirAsia
Thai Airways
Thai Smile
Turkish Cargo
VietJet Air
Vietnam Airlines
XiamenAir

SIEM REAP INTERNATIONAL

REP | VDSR

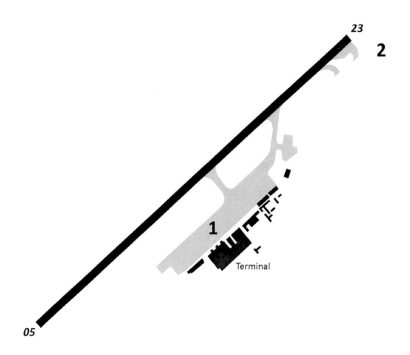

The second largest airport in Cambodia, but the busiest by the number of movements. Siem Reap handles a good selection of flights across the Far East to neighbouring countries, and is an important tourist gateway to the country. Chinese carriers are quite common, but operate largely during the night time hours.

The airport is a few miles from the centre of the city. It has one runway, with landings on 05 and departures on 23 so as not to disturb the important Angkor Wat temple nearby.

BASE FOR:
Cambodia Angkor Air
Sky Angkor Airlines

↓

CAMBODIA

Spotting Locations

1. Terminal
Aircraft park remotely with no air bridges, so passengers get a good view when travelling to or from their aircraft, however the views from within the terminal are not as good because of this. After security in the international terminal you have a good viewpoint.

2. Runway 23 Lineup
The road leading north from the terminal area passes close by the end of runway 23. You have great views of aircraft lining up for departure here, with photography best on the morning.

You'll need a car, or to hire a driver to take you there.

REGULAR:
AirAsia
Air Busan
Air Seoul
Bangkok Airways
Bassanka Air
Beijing Capital
Cathay Dragon
Cebu Pacific
China Eastern
China Southern
Far Eastern Air Transport
HK Express
GX Airlines
Hainan Airlines
Jetstar Asia
Jetstar Pacific
JC International
Lanmei Airlines
Lao Airlines
Malaysia Airlines
Shandong Airlines
SilkAir
Spring Airlines
Thai AirAsia
Thai Smile
VietJet Air
Vietnam Airlines
XiamenAir

OTHER AIRPORTS

Sihanoukville International

KOS | VDSV

Third largest airport in Cambodia, mostly handling domestic flights as well as some Chinese and Malaysian routes by the likes of AirAsia, Hainan Airlines and Lanmei Airlines.

The airport has a single runway and small terminal and parking area at the northern end. There are some views from the car park outside, as well as from within the terminal.

If you visit the nearby city, look out for an Antonov An-24 perched on top of an apartment building in Victory Hill.

CHINA

Capital: Beijing

Overview

China's growth on the world stage has coincided with massive development of its aviation industry. There are now many regional and international airlines operating in the country, both full service and low-cost carriers. There are also hundreds of airports all over the country, with hundreds more planned over coming decades. Most existing facilities have been upgraded with new terminals and runways over recent years.

In this chapter of the book, I have not listed every airport in China as it would warrant a book in itself. In fact, most of the regional airports in the country are very similar and feature the same aircraft and airlines as any other, being linked to the major hubs around the country. The ones listed here are those which offer either a better spotting experience or something else of note.

Sadly few airports provide any official spotting locations, and I don't anticipate this to change with any of the newer airports under construction.

For the beginner to China, Beijing and Shanghai will more than suffice. These cities have large airports, with spotting locations and hotels, and fantastic museums to visit.

Soon, Beijing's new Daxing Airport will open, changing the landscape of the city's airports from what is described here (keep an eye on www.airportspotting.com for updates). What it offers the spotter is as yet unknown.

PRINCIPAL AIRPORTS

BEIJING CAPITAL INTERNATIONAL

PEK | ZBAA

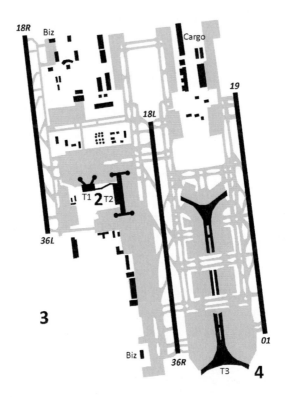

Beijing Capital is currently the principal airport for the city, and has been steadily expanded and modernised, but is soon to be overshadowed by the new Daxing Airport (Capital will remain open, however).

Capital, 20 miles north of the city, is a large hub where domestic and international flights meet, and it is currently the busiest in Asia, and second-busiest airport in the world. It has three parallel runways, and the very large international Terminal 3 to the east.

BASE FOR:
Air China
Beijing Capital
China Eastern
China Southern
Hainan Airlines
Shandong Airlines
Shenzhen Airlines
Sichuan Airlines

↓

Terminals 1 and 2 are to the west, with areas for maintenance and Chinese Air Force operations to the north and west.

This is one of the better airports for spotting at in China, which is useful considering the sheer number of aircraft which pass through daily. It also has a good hotel for spotting.

Many enthusiasts come to Beijing for the famous Datan Shan aviation museum, which is a short distance north of Capital Airport and well worth the visit for any classic airliner fans.

Spotting Locations

1. Viewing Mound at West Lake Park
This dedicated area is situated under the final approach to runway 36R. It is elevated, with views over the western side of the airfield, Terminal 3, and the nearby executive apron. Photography is good from this spot, which is reached by walking along the twisting path from the terminal. Alternatively, you can reach the spot by road.

2. Domestic Terminals
Inside the Domestic Terminal you're free to roam around and enjoy the views from the windows of all the domestic airlines here. Photography is acceptable from here (through glass), and you can see across to Terminal 3.

3. Tianbei Road
For good shots of arrivals on runway 36L (the most westerly runway), Tianbei Road has a couple of good locations including a pedestrian overpass, and a grass area near the junction with Tianzhu Street. You'll need a taxi to take you here, either heading to or from the airport. Simply move either side of the approach as the sun moves.

REGULAR:
Aeroflot
Aigle Azur
AirBridgeCargo
Air Algerie
Air Astana
Air Canada
Air France
Air Hong Kong
Air Koryo
Air Macau
AirAsia X
All Nippon Airways
American Airlines
Asiana Airlines
Austrian Airlines
Azerbaijan Airlines
British Airways
Cambodia Angkor Air
Cargolux
Cathay Dragon
Cathay Pacific
Cebu Pacific
China Airlines
China Postal Airlines
Dalian Airlines
Delta
Donghai Airlines
EgyptAir
El Al
Emirates
Ethiopian Airlines
Etihad
EVA Air
FedEx Express
Finnair
Garuda Indonesia
Grand China Air
Hong Kong Airlines
Iraqi Airways
Japan Airlines
Jeju Air
Juneyao Airlines
KLM
Korean Air
Loong Air
LOT Polish Airlines
Lucky Air
Lufthansa
Mahan Air

↓

4. Terminal 3 Car Park

For great views of aircraft landing on runway 01, head to the car park on the eastern side of Terminal 3's main entrance (at ground level). You should not be bothered here if you keep you actions discrete.

Spotting Hotel

Cordis Beijing Capital Airport

1 Yijing Road, Terminal 3, Capital International Airport, Beijing 100621 | +86 10 6457 5555
beijingairport.langhamplacehotels.com

The best spotting hotel at Beijing Capital is the Cordis (formerly the Langham Place). It is situated close to Terminal 3 and has rooms facing the runways, city skyline, or the lake. Rooms facing the runway look over the approach to runway 01, whilst those facing the lake will have views of aircraft approaching runway 36R, with 36L in the distance. Windows in the corridor offer views of aircraft on opposite runways. When aircraft are landing from the north the views are not as good. The hotel is a 10-15 minute walk from spotting location 1.

Malaysia Airlines
MIAT Mongolian Airlines
NordStar Airlines
Pakistan International
Philippine Airlines
Qantas
Qatar Airways
S7 Airlines
Scandinavian Airlines
SF Airlines
Singapore Airlines
SriLankan Airlines
Swiss International
Tajik Air
Thai Airways
Tibet Airlines
Turkmenistan Airlines
Turkish Airlines
Ukraine International
United Airlines
Ural Airlines
Uzbekistan Airways
Vietnam Airlines
XiamenAir

CHENGDU SHUANGLIU INTERNATIONAL

CTU | ZUUU

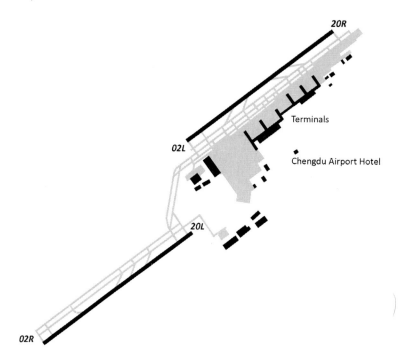

A large airport in central China, Chengdu acts as a hub for the west of the country, with many domestic links. It is also served by international carriers from Europe, the Middle East and North America. Chengdu Airlines and Sichuan Airlines are headquartered here and have maintenance facilities at the airport.

BASE FOR:
Air China
Chengdu Airlines
China Eastern
China Southern
Lucky Air
Shenzhen Airlines
Sichuan Airlines
Tibet Airlines

REGULAR:
AirAsia X
AirBridgeCargo Airlines
Air Macau
Air Mauritius
All Nippon Airways
Asiana Airlines
↓

The airport has a pair of parallel runways which are staggered, with the terminal area alongside the northern runway 02L/20R. A large apron used by cargo flights and commuter aircraft stretches south of the terminals.

The only known spotting locations are within the terminal, where some views are available landside, as well as from the airside gate areas.

Spotting Hotel

Chengdu Airport Hotel
Shuangliu Int'l Airport, Shuangliu County, Chengdu

Even-numbered rooms on the top three floors (the 10th floor is for family rooms) have good views facing the northern runway. You can't see any aircraft parking stands or the southern runway, but should see most movements.

Bangkok Airways
Beijing Capital
Cathay Dragon
Cathay Pacific Cargo
China Airlines
China Cargo Airlines
China Express Airlines
China Postal Airlines
China United
Colorful Guizhou Airlines
DHL
Donghai Airlines
Ethiopian Airlines
Etihad
EVA Air
Far Eastern Air Transport
FedEx Express
Garuda Indonesia
GX Airlines
Hainan Airlines
Hebei Airlines
Hong Kong Airlines
Hongtu Airlines
Juneyao Airlines
KLM
Korean Air Cargo
Kunming Airlines
Lao Airlines
Lion Air
Loong Air
Lufthansa Cargo
Malindo Air
Nok Air
Okay Airways
PAL Express
Qatar Airways
Qingdao Airlines
Ruili Airlines
SF Airlines
Shandong Airlines
Shenzhen Donghai Airlines
SilkAir
Sky Angkor Airlines
Spring Airlines
Thai AirAsia
Thai Airways
Thai Lion Air
Tianjin Airlines
United Airlines
UPS Airlines
Urumqi Air
Vietnam Airlines
XiamenAir
Yangtze River Express

GUANGZHOU BAIYUN INTERNATIONAL

CAN | ZGGG

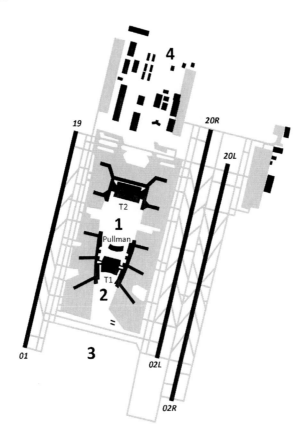

Guangzhou Baiyun International is China's third-busiest airport and a major hub in the south of the country. It opened in August 2004, replacing the previous airport of the same name which had outgrown its crowded city location. The current airport has three parallel runways and a large central terminal complex with the six-pier Terminal 1, and even larger Terminal 2, which opened in April 2018, as a home to the based China Southern Airlines and its partners.

BASE FOR:
9 Air
China Eastern
China Southern
FedEx Express
Hainan Airlines
Shenzhen Airlines

↓

Since 2008 the airport has also been the Asia-Pacific hub for FedEx Express and handles hundreds of flights per week from the dedicated cargo complex on the northern part of the airport. Many other cargo airlines also visit.

Guangzhou is not an easy airport for spotters. The Pullman Hotel is a good option.

It's worth taking a trip to the nearby technical institute (4) on the northern perimeter of the airport, which is home to a variety of historic airliners used as instructional airframes, including Tridents, MD-80s, IL-14s and Y-7s. Try to arrange a visit in advance if you want access to take pictures.

Spotting Locations

1. Terminals
Airside in the terminals there are plenty of windows through which parked aircraft and movements can be observed. However, the number of aircraft that can be seen is limited to whichever side of the terminal you are in.

2. Car Park A1
You can see aircraft departing from this car park situated close to Terminal 1. Security have been known to move spotters on from here, however.

3. Cross Taxiway
South of the terminal a taxiway crosses between both sides of the airport. Cross 8th Road runs parallel to this with some good views of aircraft taxying by. It is within walking distance of the hotels to the south of the airport.

REGULAR:
Aeroflot
AirAsia
Air China
Air France
Air Madagascar
All Nippon Airways
Asiana Airlines
Bangkok Airways
Beijing Capital
Cambodia Angkor Air
Cathay Dragon
Cebu Pacific
Chengdu Airlines
China Airlines
China Postal Airlines
China United
Chongqing Airlines
EgyptAir
Emirates
Ethiopian Airlines
Etihad Cargo
EVA Air
FedEx Express
Finnair
Garuda Indonesia
GX Airlines
Hebei Airlines
Japan Airlines
Jetstar Pacific
Juneyao Airlines
Kenya Airways
Korean Air
Kunming Airlines
Lanmei Airlines
Lao Airlines
Loong Air
Lufthansa Cargo
Mahan Air
Malaysia Airlines
Malindo Air
Myanmar Airways International
Okay Airways
Oman Air
Philippine Airlines
Philippines AirAsia
Qatar Airways
Saudia
Scoot
SF Airlines

↓

Spotting Hotel

Pullman Hotel

Guangzhou Baiyun Airport, 510470 | +86 20 3606 8866 |
www.pullmanhotels.com

Club rooms on the higher floors of this hotel have
good views of the runways, which is especially
useful if aircraft are landing towards you. If the
opposite direction is in use you will see aircraft
departing past you. Some parking aprons and the
distant FedEx ramp are also visible.

Shandong Airlines
Sichuan Airlines
Singapore Airlines
Spring Airlines
Sriwijaya Air
Thai AirAsia
Thai Airways
Thai Lion Air
Thai Smile
Tianjin Airlines
Turkish Airlines
Uni Air
US-Bangla Airlines
Vietnam Airlines
West Air
XiamenAir
Yangtze River Express

SHANGHAI HONGQIAO INTERNATIONAL

SHA | ZSSS

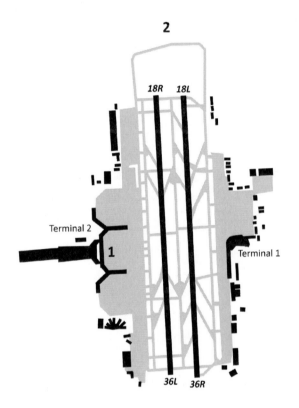

Hongqiao was Shanghai's main airport until 1999 when the new Pudong Airport to the east of the city opened, relieving some of the strain. Despite this, Hongqiao remains in the top ten busiest airports in China and is very convenient for the city centre. It is mainly a domestic airport, although some international flights operate to neighbouring Asian countries. It is the home base of China Eastern Airlines.

BASE FOR:
China Eastern
Juneyao Airlines
Shanghai Airlines
Spring Airlines

↓

The airport layout involves a pair of north-south parallel runways with passenger terminal areas on the western side, and cargo, corporate and maintenance areas on the eastern side.

For spotters, it is good to spend time at both Shanghai airports to make sure you catch aircraft that don't operate from both.

Spotting Locations

1. Terminal 2
While an observation deck was constructed on Terminal 2, it is no longer open. There is a café area alongside its entrance, however, with some views over the airport.

2. Tianshan Road
If you alight the Metro (line 2) one stop before the airport (Songhong Road), then walk to the west along Tianshan W Road, you'll come to a position under the approach to runway 18L/R after about 15 minutes' walk. Position yourself with regards to the sun and the runway in use for good approach shots.

3. Terminal 1
The windows in the domestic Terminal 1 are great for viewing traffic and photographing aircraft parked close to you. You will not see much at the distant Terminal 2 from here, but aircraft on the runway are visible if you pick your spot.

REGULAR:
Air China
Air Macau
All Nippon Airways
Asiana Airlines
Cathay Dragon
Chengdu Airlines
China Airlines
China Southern
China United
EVA Air
Hainan Airlines
Hebei Airlines
Hong Kong Airlines
Japan Airlines
Korean Air
Lucky Air
Shandong Airlines
Shenzhen Airlines
Tianjin Airlines
Tibet Airlines
XiamenAir

Spotting Hotels

Hong Gang Shanghai Hotel

2550 Hongqiao Road, Shanghai 200335 | +86 21 6268 1008

Ask for a high room with number ending in 10–910 for example is a good room. Others include 606 and 702. These all face the terminal's parking ramps and are perfect for spotting and photography. The hotel is very reasonably priced.

Boyue Shanghai Hongqiao Airport (Air China) Hotel

No.181, Shen Da San Road, Hongqiao Airport, Shanghain 200335 | +86 21 2236 6666
www.zhboyuehotel.com

Situated in Terminal 2, if you get an Executive room on floors 9 and above you have excellent views of movements. You'll see aircraft parked at both of the terminals, plus runway movements and the executive ramp.

Public Transport

Travel between Shanghai Hongqiao and Pudong airports is easy. The Airport Shuttle Bus line 1 runs direct between the two airports, taking just under an hour.

SHANGHAI PUDONG INTERNATIONAL

PVG | ZSPD

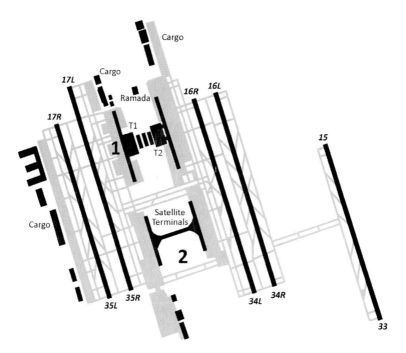

Shanghai Pudong International opened in 1999, replacing the older Hongqiao Airport which was no longer able to expand. Situated around 20 miles east of the city, Pudong is now one of Asia's busiest hubs.

The airport has five parallel runways and two passenger terminals in the centre; it is also a large cargo hub with various ramps on the north, south and western side of the airport dedicated to this.

BASE FOR:
Air China
China Cargo Airlines
China Eastern
China Southern
DHL Aviation
FedEx Express
Hainan Airlines
Juneyao Airlines
Shanghai Airlines
Spring Airlines
Suparna Airlines
UPS Airlines

↓

Unfortunately, Pudong wasn't built with the enthusiast in mind. No dedicated viewing facilities are provided, and very few views through terminal windows are possible without passing through security. What's more, the roads around the airport do not offer many views. Because of this, many spotters have better luck by booking a room in one of the airport hotels which overlook the action.

The majority of movements at Pudong are international. Therefore, if you want to see domestic airlines whilst in Shanghai, you should visit Hongqiao Airport.

Buses run to Hongqiao Airport from Pudong on a regular basis from outside domestic arrivals. It is useful to visit both airports as many aircraft in the fleets of the bigger carriers do not visit both.

Spotting Locations

1. International Terminal
There are windows in the terminal with some views of aircraft on the international side of the airport. Head up to departures level and walk to the end alongside the coffee shop. Be discrete as some security officers like to move spotters on.

2. Southerly Arrivals
If aircraft are arriving on the 35L/R runways, you can walk south from the terminal along the road and find a spot which has views. Photography isn't very good from this area, but at least you can log most arrivals.

REGULAR:
Aeroflot
AeroLogic
Aeromexico
AirAsia X
AirBridgeCargo
Air Canada
Air France
Air Hong Kong
Air India
Air Koryo
Air Macau
Air Mauritius
Air New Zealand
All Nippon Airways
American Airlines
Asiana Airlines
ASL Airlines Belgium
Atlas Air
Austrian Airlines
Beijing Capital
British Airways
Cambodia Angkor Air
Cargolux
Cathay Dragon
Cathay Pacific
Cebu Pacific
Chengdu Airlines
China Airlines
China Postal Airlines
Chongqing Airlines
Dalian Airlines
Delta
Donghai Airlines
Eastar Jet
Emirates
Ethiopian Airlines
Etihad
EVA Air
Finnair
Fuzhou Airlines
Garuda Indonesia
Hebei Airlines
Hong Kong Airlines
Iberia
Iran Air Cargo
Japan Airlines
Jetstar Japan
Jin Air

↓

Spotting Hotels

Dazhong Merrylin 'Ease' Hotel Pudong Airport

6001 Yingbin Avenue, Pudong New Area, Shanghai 201202
+86 21 3879 9999 | www.dazhongairporthotel.com

This hotel is reasonably priced and has a direct link to the terminal and train station. Rooms on higher floors facing south have views over the taxiways and runways. An SBS is useful for night movements. Rooms 8801, 8802 and 8806 are reportedly good

Ramada Pudong Airport Shanghai

1100 Qi Hang Road, Shanghai 201207 | +86 21 3849 4949
www.ramada.com

This hotel is also reasonably priced but offers fewer spotting opportunities. Again, ask for a south facing room looking towards the airport, and on a high floor. You will then get distant views of runway movements and terminal views.

Kalitta Air
KLM
Korean Air
Kunming Airlines
Lion Air
Lucky Air
Lufthansa
Mahan Air
Malaysia Airlines
MNG Airlines
National Airlines
Nippon Cargo
Peach
Philippine Airlines
Philippines AirAsia
Polar Air Cargo
Qantas
Qatar Airways
Royal Brunei
S7 Airlines
Saudia Cargo
Scandinavian Airlines
SF Airlines
Shandong Airlines
Silk Way Airlines
Singapore Airlines
Southern Air
SriLankan Airlines
Swiss International
Thai AirAsia X
Thai Airways
Thai Lion Air
Tianjin Airlines
Turkish Airlines
T'way Airlines
United Airlines
Vietnam Airlines
Virgin Atlantic
Volga-Dnepr Airlines
West Air
XiamenAir

SHENZHEN BAO'AN INTERNATIONAL

SZX | ZGSZ

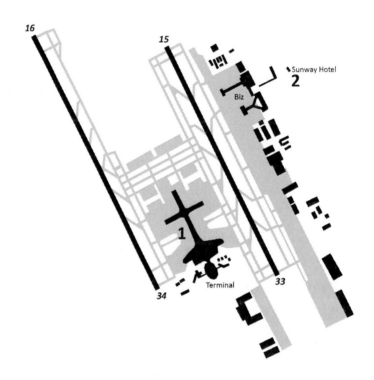

A part of the hugely important concentration of population in the south of China which includes Hong Kong, Macau and Guangzhou, Shenzhen Bao'an International has grown significantly over recent years.

The airport has two runways, and in 2013 opened a large, modern terminal in the central area to replace the three older facilities. The former passenger terminals on the north side are now used by corporate jets.

BASE FOR:
China Southern
Donghai Airlines
Hainan Airlines
Shenzhen Airlines
UPS Airlines

↓

Shenzhen is China's fifth busiest airport, and since the area is a large centre for manufacturing, the airport handles a lot of cargo flights (it is a UPS Airlines hub) in addition to the large range of passenger airlines with flights across China and the rest of the Far East.

It is possible to take a ferry direct from Bao'an Airport to Hong Kong Airport.

Spotting Locations

1. Terminal
Once airside in the terminal there are plenty of gates with good windows to view movements.

2. Sunway Hotel
With a dedicated spotter package, probably the easiest place to spot at Shenzhen (see later).

Spotting Hotel

Sunway Hotel

Shenzhen Bao'an Airport | +86 755 2730 0888
www.sunwayhotelsz.com

Located outside the original terminals A and B. Even numbered rooms on floors 3 and above face the airport which are quite distant, but take in most movements. This is probably the easiest place to spot at Shenzhen if you aren't in the departures lounge, and hotel staff are aware of the needs of spotters. Ask about the Plane Spotters Package which includes a high-floor room.

REGULAR:
AirAsia
Air China
Asiana Airlines
ASL Airlines Belgium
Cardig Air
Chengdu Airlines
China Airlines
China Eastern
Chongqing Airlines
China United
Dalian Airlines
Donghai Airlines
EVA Air Cargo
FedEx Express
I-Fly
Hebei Airlines
Juneyao Airlines
Korean Air
Kunming Airlines
Lion Air
Loong Air
Lucky Air
Lufthansa Cargo
Okay Airways
Philippines AirAsia
Scoot
SF Airlines
Shandong Airlines
Sichuan Airlines
SilkAir
Spring Airlines
Suparna Airlines
Thai AirAsia
Thai Lion Air
Tibet Airlines
Transmile Air Services
Uni Air
Uni-Top Airlines
UPS Airlines
West Air
XiamenAir
Yangtze River Express

OTHER AIRPORTS

Beijing Nanyuan Airport

NAY | ZBNY

Nanyuan is a mixed civil, military and government airport located close to the centre of Beijing. It will close in 2019 once the new Daxing Airport opens.

Nanyuan is the oldest airport in China, having opened in 1910. Nanyuan is a moderately busy domestic airport and airbase, with the sole passenger operator being China United Airlines.

The airport has a single runway and small passenger terminal. To the north and south of the passenger ramp are parking areas for government and military aircraft. Of note to the enthusiast are stored Boeing 737s and Tupolev TU-154s here, and a small collection of preserved military aircraft (including transports) located just north of the passenger terminal, but armed guards often stand between you and the aircraft, so it is not advised to stop. With Nanyuan being a military airport, it is not advisable to try and take photographs around the terminal or the guards that can be found in most areas.

Inside the passenger terminal you can read off any aircraft on the civil ramp with ease, but beware of patrolling guards. You cannot read off any movements from within the terminal.

Driving (or walking) north from the terminal will pass the northern military apron. You can get fleeting glimpses of aircraft parked here through the tress. On your right is the collection of stored and preserved aircraft at the small museum.

Changsha Huanghua International

CSX | ZGHA

Changsha is a growing airport, having recently opened a new terminal and runway, and commenced long-haul flights to Europe and North America. It has ambitions to grow further with a third runway and terminal. China Southern and Hainan Airlines have a focus here.

Both terminals have good views once airside but are limited for spotting in landside areas.

Chongqing Jiangbei International

CKG | ZUCK

What was a smaller regional airport is now a very large hub in western China. Chongqing has three parallel runways, with a fourth planned.

The centrepiece is the modern Terminal 3 in the centre of the airfield, with the older Terminal 2 and (now closed) Terminal 1 on the western side, along with cargo facilities, maintenance and corporate jet parking.

There are landside views in Terminal 2, and you can walk down to the cargo area from here. However, the new terminal has no landside views. Both terminals have good views from the airside departure areas.

Air China, China Express Airlines and Sichuan Airlines dominate the movements. However, airlines from across Asia, plus some from Europe, are regulars.

The Rica Hotel at 95 Binggang Road is situated alongside the airport and near local shopping mall and food amenities. Rooms in the ranges 919-933 and 1019-1033 offer great views over the western parallel runways, with balconies.

Fuzhou Changle International

FOC | ZSFZ

Fuzhou has a single runway and terminal, with plenty of windows airside, but no viewing areas around the terminal. If you venture to the opposite side of the runway (you'll require a car or taxi), there's an area of raised ground next to the fire station overlooking the airport.

Mostly a domestic and regional airport, with Fuzhou Airlines and XiamenAir in abundance.

Guiyang Longdongbao International

KWE | ZUGY

Guiyang is a moderately busy airport handling around 15 million passengers per year, mostly on domestic flights. Colorful Guizhou Airlines is based here.

There are views from landside in the domestic terminal between the two piers, and from all gate areas once airside.

Hangzhou Xiaoshan International

HGH | ZSHC

The principle airport in the Yangtze River Delta region, Hangzhou has a modern international terminal and two domestic terminals, situated between the two runways. It is the home base of Loong Air and a hub for a number of other Chinese carriers, including Air China, Beijing Capital, China Eastern, China Southern, Hainan Airlines and XiamenAir.

Maintenance, cargo and a large apron for corporate jets can be found in the western portion of the airport.

The airport unfortunately has a reputation of clamping down on spotters (there are views from outside the terminal departures level). So, it is best to secure a room at the ZTG Grand Hotel (www.grandairporthangzhou.com) where a top floor room can offer sweeping views over the airport.

Jinan Yaoqiang International

TNA | ZSJN

Home of Shandong Airlines and a technical area and storage facility to the north of the terminal. Jinan handles around 11 million passengers per year, and has few views from outside. However, once airside you can see all gates and movements.

The Jinan Airport Hotel has views of parts of the terminal apron, and of the runway movements.

Kunming Changshui International

KMG | ZPPP

One of the world's top 50 busiest airports, Kunming is a hub for China Eastern, China Southern, Kunming Airlines, Lucky Air, Ruili Airlines, and Sichuan Airlines. Other flights mostly link the airport to domestic and Far Eastern cities.

The airport opened in 2011 and features a large, modern terminal between parallel runways.

At departures level outside the terminal you have views at either end over the runway thresholds. Inside there is also a food court at either end with similar views. Security is usually relaxed.

The Best Yue Hang Hotel has limited views of the airport from top floor rooms, but nearly all movements can be seen.

Nanjing Lukou International

NKG | ZSNJ

Nanjing has two runways and two terminals. It is a hub for China Eastern and Shenzhen Airlines, plus China Postal Airlines which operates from a large dedicated facility to the west. Other cargo airlines use facilities to the east of the terminals.

There are some views from the departure ramp outside Terminal 2, and views are good in both terminals once airside.

Qingdao Liuting International

TAO | ZSQD

A single runway airport in the northern part of the city, with a recently-expanded terminal served by all domestic airlines (China Eastern and Shandong Airlines have bases) and some Asian and European carriers. There is a military base linked to the airport, with some preserved aircraft outside.

Views possible from within the terminal.

Also, be sure to visit the Qingdao Naval Museum in the city.

Sanya Phoenix International

SYX | ZJSY

An airport on the island of Hainan off the southern coast of China. It is served by all major Chinese airlines, with Beijing Capital, China Southern, Hainan Airlines and Sichuan Airlines having a larger presence. Other international carriers from around Asia also fly in regularly.

The airport has a single, long runway and both domestic and international passenger terminals. Many aircraft park on remote stands away from the terminal, so flying in may necessitate a useful bus journey through the parked aircraft. An apron for executive aircraft is at the eastern end of the airport.

Only fleeting glimpses are possible around the airport perimeter, for those who have access to a car. Within the terminal airside area there are good views of the nearer gates and runway.

Tianjin Binhai International

TSN | ZBTJ

Tianjin, in north east China, is an interesting airport for spotters as home to a final assembly line for the Airbus A320 family aircraft. The airport is also the home base of Okay Airways and Tianjin Airlines.

Other carriers include Air China, Asiana, EVA Air, Far Eastern Air Transport, Japan Airlines, Korean Air, Lion Air, NokScoot, Thai Lion Air and Tibet Airlines, among the usual Chinese carriers. There is also a significant cargo operation, which operates from the western side of the airport, as well as a large corporate apron where biz jet aircraft park.

Viewing is possible from the departures level outside the terminal, where some aircraft on the cargo and corporate areas can be seen. The Airbus site in the south-east corner is not visible. Views are good airside, too.

In the south-west corner is a technical school with a number of retired airliners from China's past. These can be seen from a distance, or by employing a taxi driver to explore the side streets in the area.

Tianjin Binhai International Hotel on Xi'er Road situated on the main entrance road leading to the terminal has rooms facing the airport on higher floors which have a good view of most movements, although you have runways on either side. It's not possible to see the biz jet ramps from the hotel.

Ürümqi Diwopu International

URC | ZWWW

A busy airport in northern China, close to Mongolia and Kyrgyzstan, which handles over 20 million passengers per year from its single runway. There are four passenger terminals strung out along the southern side of the runway.

Flights are dominated by domestic airlines, in particular China Southern and the home-grown Urumqi Air, with some types not seen elsewhere in the country. Some interesting carriers from neighbouring countries also fly in.

There are views from the departure lounges of all terminals. Elsewhere, spotters need to rely on a few small gaps between the buildings.

Wuhan Tianhe International

WUH | ZHHH

Wuhan is a large hub for Air China, China Eastern, China Southern, Hainan Airlines and XiamenAir. Recent upgrades include a second runway and large terminal building which replaced the three previous terminals.

Views from the terminals are best for spotting if you walk behind the check-in desks to the large windows. There is also a large cargo terminal to the north, near the runway 22R threshold.

There are views from the terminal in the landside area where aircraft taxying to and from the runways can be seen.

Xi'an Xianyang International

XIY | ZLXY

Xi'an Xianyang is a large airport in the north west of China which has been growing steadily. It handles a large list of both passenger and cargo airlines, and is one of the top ten busiest airports in the country. It is a hub airport for China Eastern Airlines, Hainan Airlines and Joy Air.

A second runway and the new Terminal 3 were opened in 2012, which increased the capacity of the airport. Two terminals are located alongside the northern runway, whilst the third and cargo apron are alongside the southern apron.

The windows in the departure lounges of Terminal 1 and 2 are tall and clean, offering plenty of views of the apron and runway beyond.

There is also a footbridge between the terminals which is good for spotting, and is within reach of WiFi.

A large remote ramp in the northern part of the airport handles biz jets, and also a fleet of Dornier 328 aircraft which are stored there. This area is difficult to see unless you are flying in or out of the airport, however you can walk north from the terminal for about 30 minutes to get a view through the fence.

Try the Aviation Hotel, situated opposite the passenger terminal, where rooms on floors 8 and 9 are reportedly the best, and you can easily spot aircraft movements even after dark.

Xiamen Gaoqi International

XMN | ZSAM

Xiamen Gaoqi International is one of China's busiest both in terms of passengers and cargo traffic, although it is not a particularly big airport and is in a constricted location on Xiamen Island. Naturally it is a hub for XiamenAir, as well as China Eastern, China Southern and Shandong Airlines. There are some international services to destinations in Asia and Europe.

Xiamen is also home to a large maintenance base for airliners, which is located behind the terminals and largely out of view. However, you may witness aircraft coming and going from the facility.

A small road in an industrial area on the north side of the airport overlooks the threshold of runway 05. From here you can photograph aircraft approaching the runway, and also see across to the terminal gates.

Inside the terminals, once through security, you have good views from all gates of aircraft parked there and at remote stands and the runway beyond.

The Fliport Garden Hotel (www.fliport.com) is a tall hotel a few minutes' walk from the airport terminal. Ask for a room facing the airport on the top three floors and you should be able to see enough over the surrounding buildings, including the southern runway threshold and nearer parking stands.

Gaoqi International is to be replaced by a brand-new airport on Dadeng Island in the mid-2020s.

Zhengzhou Xinzheng International

CGO | ZHCC

Zhengzhou has two runways and a modern passenger terminal opened in 2015. The original terminal is currently decommissioned awaiting future expansion of the airport. Most flights here are domestic or intra-Asia.

In the western part of the airport is a large cargo terminal which sees large freighters in regularly and is a focus hub for Cargolux in Asia.

There are no easy spotting locations around the airport. Aircraft movements can be seen from departures level outside the terminal, and there are good views once airside.

MUSEUMS

Beijing Civil Aviation Museum

200 Capital Airport Side Rd, Chaoyang Qu, Beijing Shi | www.caacmuseum.cn

One of a few good aviation museums in the Beijing area. This one is located a few miles southeast of Capital Airport. Its collection includes airliners such as an Airbus A310, BAe 146, HS.121 Trident and lots of Yunshuji Y-7 and Y-11s, among others. Open Tue-Sun, 9am-4.30pm

China Aviation Museum (Datangshan)

Xiaotangshan, Chan Ping County, Beijing | +86 10 6178 4882

A must-see aviation attraction in China, located around 15 miles north east of Capital Airport. The museum is home to a large number of airliner, transport and military aircraft in various states (many are fully preserved). These include HS121 Tridents, Ilyushin IL-18, Douglas DC-8, Vickers Viscount, many Lisunov Li-2's, MiG's, Shenyang F-5's and Ilyushin IL-10's. Over 200 aircraft can be found here. The museum is open Tuesday to Sunday from 8am to 5.30pm. Entrance is 40 Yuan for adults. Bus 912 runs from Andingmen Station to the gate of the museum, but a taxi from your hotel is often best.

Qingdao Naval Museum

8 Laiyang Rd, Shinan Qu, Qingdao Shi, Shandong Sheng | +86 532 8286 6784

Located next to the naval base in the docks area of Qingdao. This museum includes a variety of aircraft linked to the Chinese Navy over the years, including an Antonov An-24 and Ilyushin Il-14. Open 8.30am-5.30pm.

HONG KONG

Capital: Hong Kong

HONG KONG
CHEK LAP KOK

Overview

Officially part of China, but still a separate entity which is a big draw
to aviation enthusiasts. The old Kai Tak airport in Kowloon Bay with its
curving approach is long gone, but the modern replacement is a busy hub
for passenger and cargo aircraft. It has facilities for enthusiasts and enough
variation to keep you interested.

Getting around Hong Kong and to the airport is also easy, with the Airport
Express train, plus bus and taxi options. You can buy an Octopus card from
customer service offices at stations and top it up to allow travel on public
transport, including ferries, buses, MTR and trains. It can also be used to pay
in some shops, cinemas and car parks.

PRINCIPAL AIRPORTS

HONG KONG CHEK LAP KOK INTERNATIONAL

HKG | VHHH

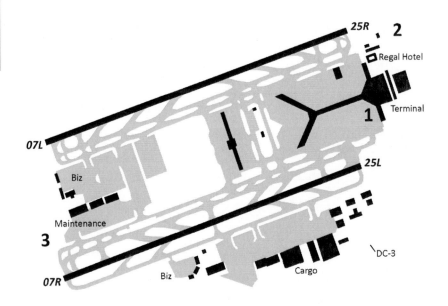

Hong Kong's current airport is to the west of the city, built on reclaimed land to replace the famous Kai Tak airport in 1998. The new airport is much more spacious and modern and has two runways and a large central terminal complex. This will be added to with an additional terminal and runway in the coming years.

To complement the terminal, which is on the eastern side of the airport, there are sizeable maintenance areas to the west, and cargo apron located on the southern side of the airport. A centre for business jet is also on the southern side.

Hong Kong is always busy and a pleasure to spot at, with an official spotting location and good

BASE FOR:
Air Hong Kong
Cathay Pacific
Cathay Dragon
DHL Aviation
Hong Kong Airlines
HK Express
UPS Airlines

↓

spotting hotels. Traffic is dominated by Cathay Pacific and Asian carriers, operating mainly wide-body airliners.

The airport is the world's busiest for cargo, with freighters taking up a good portion of movements.

Spotting Locations

1. Sky Deck
This official location is on top of Terminal 2 is the Sky Deck. It is accessed via the Aviation Discovery Centre, and you require a ticket to enter (bought from the cinema entrance, priced HKD15). This is a good location for an overall view of movements, and you won't really miss anything going on at the airport. It is good for photographing arrivals on runway 25R until late afternoon, although aircraft on the ground can be too distant. The deck is open weekdays from 11am-10pm, and weekends from 9.30am-10pm. There are no facilities on the deck, but you can head back downstairs for refreshment and toilet facilities.

2. Alternative 25R
An alternative location to the Sky Deck for runway 25R arrivals is the corner of Cheong Yip Rd and Cheong Wing Rd, which is still close enough to the terminal to be convenient, but free to use and not restricted by opening times. It is great for photographs of arriving aircraft. To reach it, leave the terminal and walk north past the taxi rank. Be careful as there is a security post nearby.

2. Maintenance Areas
At the extreme western side of the airport, there are a number locations near the maintenance hangars which are great for watching and photographing arrivals and departures. You can also log aircraft parked in this area. It is a long walk from the terminals, so take a car or the S52 bus (destination Aircraft Maintenance Area) from Tung Chung. The S1 bus runs from the terminal to Tung Chung. Look out for a preserved Douglas DC-3 which you will pass on the bus.

REGULAR:
Aeroflot
AirAsia
Air Astana
AirBridgeCargo
Air Busan
Air Canada
Air China
Air France
Air India
Air Mauritius
Air New Zealand
Air Niugini
Air Seoul
All Nippon Airways
American Airlines
Asiana
ASL Airlines
Austrian Airlines
Bangkok Airways
British Airways
Cambodia Angkor Air
Cargolux
Cebu Pacific
China Airlines
China Eastern
China Southern
Delta
DHL Aviation
Donghai Airlines
Eastar Jet
EgyptAir
El Al
Emirates
Ethiopian Airlines
Etihad
EVA Air
FedEx Express
Fiji Airways
Finnair
Garuda
Japan Airlines
JC International
Jeju Air
Jet Airways
Jetstar Asia
Jetstar Japan
Jetstar Pacific
Jin Air
Juneyao Airlines

↓

Spotting Hotels

Regal Airport Hotel

9 Cheong Tat Road, Hong Kong International Airport,
Hong Kong | +825 2276 8888 | www.regalhotel.com

This hotel is linked to the terminal building and
some rooms have excellent views of aircraft,
especially on runway 25R. Be sure to ask for a
room with views of the airport, and higher up if
possible (1140, 1142, 1146, 1148 are all good).
The hotel is expensive, but is comfortable and has
the benefit of the views and a restaurant which
also overlooks the aprons and runways.

Marriott Skycity Hotel

1 SkyCity Road East, Hong Kong International Airport,
Lantau Hong Kong | +852 3969 1888 | www.marriott.com

Rooms in this hotel offer fantastic views, and
it's only a short walk from the terminal and the
Skydeck viewing area. Even numbered rooms
high up offer views of short finals to runway 07R,
and some views of the cargo ramp. Flight tracking
software will be needed at night.

K-Mile Air
KLM
Korean Air
Lanmei Airlines
Lufthansa
Malaysia Airlines
Malindo Air
Mandarin Airlines
MIAT Mongolian
Myanmar National
National Airlines
Nepal Airlines
Peach
Philippine Airlines
Philippines AirAsia
Qantas
Qatar Airways
Royal Brunei
Royal Jordanian
S7 Airlines
SAS
Saudia Cargo
Scoot
Shandong Airlines
Shenzhen Airlines
Siam Air
Sichuan Airlines
Silk Way Airlines
Singapore Airlines
South African Airways
Spring Airlines
SriLankan
Swiss International
Thai AirAsia
Thai Airways
Transmile Air
Tri-MG
Turkish Airlines
T'way Airlines
ULS Cargo
United Airlines
Vanilla Air
VietJet Air
Vietnam Airlines
Virgin Atlantic
Virgin Australia
XiamenAir
Yangtze River Express

MUSEUMS

Hong Kong Science Museum

2 Science Museum Rd, Tsim Sha Tsui East, Hong Kong | hk.science.museum

Hundreds of hands-on exhibits covering all sorts of topics. For enthusiasts, you will want to see the preserved Cathay Pacific Douglas DC-3, VR-HDB. Open daily except Thursday, 10am-7pm (9pm on weekends).

INDIA

Capital: New Delhi

Overview

It is fair to say that few spotters these days go on a dedicated trip to India as the country is known to be against such activities. In fact, spotters in recent years have been arrested or questioned, even in the comfort of their hotel room, so it goes without saying that discretion is advised. No airports as yet provide official spotting areas.

Nevertheless, India's size and population means it is a country with a sizeable aviation infrastructure, including airports that are steadily modernizing and airlines with growing fleets and improving levels of service. Many more regional airports are expected to be built across the country in coming decades.

Despite the restrictions, there is an active aviation enthusiast community in India and many great pictures surface from the locations people do access. The official line is that photography is permitted at all civilian airports. You are also permitted to take photographs on board and airliner, so long as you are a ticket holder on that flight, and the aircraft is not at a government or military airport.

Another key aspect of the rules to remember if you are photographing outside an airport – it is not permitted to take pictures of the airport itself, however there is no rules about pictures at the airport.

DELHI INDIRA GANDHI INTERNATIONAL

DEL | VIDP

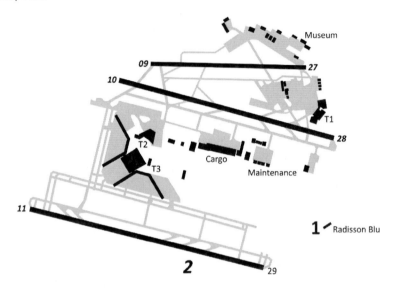

India's largest and busiest airport, and home to most of the nation's airlines.

The airport has three active runways. The original Terminal 1 is to the north, whilst terminals 2 and 3 are in a central area. A further three terminals are in the planning stages, along with a fourth runway.

To the east of the central area you'll find busy cargo facilities and maintenance areas for Air India and a number of stored Indian Air Force aircraft.

To the north, alongside the shorter runway, is the military base, and a small Air Force Museum (see later).

The tall concrete walls around Delhi Airport makes exploring the perimeter difficult, and

BASE FOR:
AirAsia India
Air India
Alliance Air
GoAir
IndiGo
Jet Airways
Quikjet Airlines
SpiceJet
Vistara
Zoom Air

REGULAR:
Aeroflot
Air Arabia
Air Astana
Air Canada
Air China
Air France
Air India Express
Air Manas
↓

the city's heat and pollution can make any photographs you do take look hazy.

Your safest bet for spotting here is to obtain a room at the Radisson Blu hotel (1), but be aware that this is where spotters were arrested after their equipment aroused suspicion to a cleaner.

Another good location is along the southern perimeter where the UER II road meets the intersection with the Old Delhi Gurgaon Road (2). By the side of the road you'll often see people gathered to watch aircraft, along with food stalls and lots of rubbish. Here you can see aircraft using runway 11/29, and photography is possible.

Spotting Hotel

Radisson Blu Plaza Delhi

Near Mahipalpur Extension, Nh 8, New Delhi, 110037 | +91 11 2677 9191 | www.radissonblu.com

Situated at the eastern side of the airport near the main motorway linking it to the city. This is a large and very comfortable and western hotel. Depending on your room you should be able to see aircraft arriving on runways 27, 28 and 29, and some departures. The terminals are a little far away, and higher rooms are better for seeing over the surrounding trees.

This is the hotel where a maid reported spotters for suspicious behaviour, leading to their arrest. So caution should be taken over your activities and leaving equipment such as binoculars, cameras and SBS units on display.

Air Mauritius
Air Odisha
AirAsia X
Alitalia
All Nippon Airways
Ariana Afghan
Asiana Airlines
ASL Airlines Belgium
Bhutan Airlines
Blue Dart Aviation
British Airways
Cathay Pacific
China Airlines
China Eastern Airlines
China Southern Airlines
DHL Aviation
Druk Air
Emirates
Ethiopian Airlines
Etihad
FedEx Express
Finnair
flydubai
Gulf Air
Iraqi Airways
Japan Airlines
Kalitta Air
Kam Air
KLM
Korean Air
Kuwait Airways
Lufthansa
Mahan Air
Malaysia Airlines
Malindo Air
Meraj Airlines
Nepal Airlines
Oman Air
Pakistan International
Qatar Airways
Saudia
Singapore Airlines
Shandong Airlines
SriLankan Airlines
Swiss International
Tajik Air
Thai Airways
Turkish Airlines
Turkmenistan Airlines
Ukraine International
Uni-Top Airlines
United Airlines
Uzbekistan Airways
Virgin Atlantic
WOW air

MUMBAI CHHATRAPATI SHIVAJI INTERNATIONAL

BOM | VABB

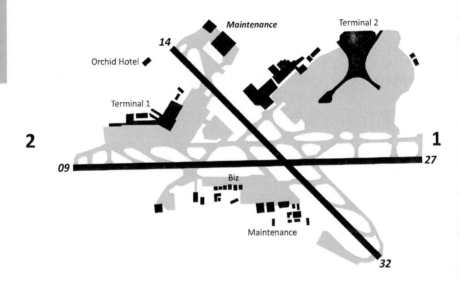

India's second largest and busiest airport, and one of the world's busiest for movements, having broken the 24-hour record twice.

Mumbai has two runways, which cross in the middle. To the north is the brand-new Terminal 2, whilst the older Terminal 1 is to the west. Air India performs maintenance on its fleet at locations around the airport site, and there's a busy general aviation and corporate hub on the southern side of the airport.

The best spotting location at Mumbai is an area of raised ground (1) alongside the threshold of runway 27. It affords incredible photographs of aircraft on the runway and taxiway, and locals often gather here. However, officials will usually interrogate or move on spotters if they

BASE FOR:
Air Deccan
Air India
Alliance Air
Blue Dart Aviation
GoAir
IndiGo
Jet Airways
SpiceJet

REGULAR:
Aerologic
Air Arabia
Air China
Air Canada
Air India Express
Air Italy

↓

pass by. You may need local assistance to reach the location, which is behind houses off Magan Nathuram Road as it passes the eastern side of the airport. The area is very dirty and smelly.

Another location is off the Western Express Highway at the 09 end of the runway (2). It is acceptable to park up at the side of the service road alongside the highway and watch (or even risk photographing) aircraft movements.

Spotting Hotels

Orchid Hotel

Adjacent to Domestic, 70-C, Nehru Rd, Vile Parle East, Mumbai, 400099 | +91 22 2616 4040

A well-known hotel for spotters at Mumbai. It is found near Terminal 1 and the runway 14 threshold. Its roof terrace has a pool and good views over this part of the airport. Security, however, is now very tight and anyone using cameras or binoculars are usually spoken to immediately. Rooms on the top floor can have great views, with 702-707 reportedly good. Anyone with access to the executive floor can use the special lounge all day, which itself has good views. Spotting is allowed, but again no cameras.

Hotel Taj

Chhatrapati Shivaji Airport (Domestic Terminal), Off Western Express Highway, Santacruz (East), Mumbai, Maharashtra 400099 | +91 22 6211 5211 | www.tajhotels.com

Quite a luxury hotel, and different from the well-established Orchid as a spotting location. The Taj is situated behind the domestic terminal, so rooms overlook the parking stands and runway beyond. Great for photography and service.

Air Mauritius
Air Seychelles
All Nippon Airways
Atlas Air
Bangkok Airways
British Airways
Brussels Airlines
Cargolux
Cathay Pacific
Druk Air
EgyptAir
El Al
Emirates
Ethiopian Airlines
Etihad
FedEx Express
flydubai
Garuda Indonesia
Gulf Air
Iran Air
Iraqi Airways
Jazeera Airways
Joon
KLM
Kenya Airways
Korean Air
Kuwait Airways
Lufthansa
Malaysia Airlines
Malindo Air
Nepal Airlines
Oman Air
Qatar Airways
Quikjet Airlines
RwandAir
Saudia
Singapore Airlines
SriLankan Airlines
Swiss International
Thai Airways
Thai Lion Air
Thai Smile
Turkish Airlines
Uni-Top Airlines
United Airlines
UPS Airlines
Uzbekistan Airways
Vistara
Yemenia

OTHER AIRPORTS

Ahmedabad Sardar Vallabhbhai Patel International

AMD | VAAH

One of India's busiest cargo airports, and home to Blue Dart Aviation. Other carriers include Emirates SkyCargo, Ethiopian Airlines Cargo, Etihad Cargo and Qatar Airways Cargo.

There are also two passenger terminals at Ahmedabad. IndiGo and SpiceJet are the busiest carriers, with some international flights.

You may have some views from the roadways between the terminals. Those with transport can also drive along Airport Road as it passes the end of runway 23. There are places to pull over and watch aircraft arrivals, and locals will be doing the same. Photography can be good, but you may be moved on.

Chennai International

MAA | VOMM

India's fourth busiest airport, handling over 20 million passengers per year. It has both domestic and international terminals side-by-side in the south-western corner of the airport, with cargo facilities to the east. To the north is remote parking and a corporate aviation terminal. The airport has two runways.

Movements are dominated by Alliance Air, Blue Dart Aviation, IndiGo, Jet Airways and SpiceJet, which has a base here. There are many international flights, including long-haul links to Europe and across Asia.

There are some views from the drop-off area outside the terminal. Another good location is the St. Thomas Mount area of the city, just east of the airport. Aircraft pass low over here on approach.

The Trident Hotel (www.tridenthotels.com) has some rooms with views of the ends of runway 25 and 30, and also has a rooftop terrace.

Goa Dabolim Airport

GOI | VOGO

This is one of India's only tourist airports, with many resorts nearby. As well as the usual domestic and low cost traffic, it sees many seasonal charters from Europe and Russia. You can also visit the nearby Naval Aviation Museum (see later).

The airport has one runway, and is also a military base so extra care must be taken. Despite what you may be told, photography is permitted within passenger terminals in India, and also on board aircraft if you have a ticket.

Locals also often congregate near Dabolim Railway Station which is close to the western end of runway 26.

Hyderabad Rajiv Gandhi International

HYD | VOHS

A new airport, opened in March 2008, to replace the older, crowded airport in the city which is now used as a training and military airfield.

The new site has a single east-west runway, and terminal to its north. It handles around 18 million passengers per year – mostly on domestic flights, but also with international services from British Airways, Emirates, Etihad, flydubai, Malaysia Airlines, Oman Air, Qatar Airways, Scoot, Saudia, SriLankan and Thai Airways. Various cargo carriers also visit, using the modest facilities to the west of the terminal.

Various quiet roads surround the airport, where locals often gather to watch movements. Aircraft are also visible from the departure lounge.

Kolkata Netaji Subhas Chandra Bose International

CCU | VECC

Another busy Indian airport. Kolkata has undergone much modernisation over recent years to deal with overcrowding and outdated facilities.

Movements are dominated by all of the main domestic carriers. Air India, IndiGo and SpiceJet are the busiest. International carriers include Biman Bangladesh, Cathay Dragon, China Eastern, Druk Air, Emirates, Etihad, Qatar Airways, Singapore Airlines, Thai Airways and US-Bangla, among others.

There are good views from the terminal departure areas. The Swissotel Kolkata (www.swissotel.com) also has reasonable views from the top three floors.

Kochi Cochin International

COK | VOCI

A brand-new, purpose build civilian airport which opened in 1999. It was built with expansion in mind, and has quickly grown to over 10 million yearly passengers. Kochi has two terminals at right-angles to each other, and a single runway (at present).

There are some views from the access roads leading to departures level outside the terminals. A road also runs along the southern perimeter of the airport, parallel to the runway, where some choose to watch aircraft from.

MUSEUMS

Air Force Museum

Palam, New Delhi, 110010 | www.indianairforce.nic.in

A collection of memorabilia and history relating to the Indian Air Force, located on the northern boundary of Delhi Airport, among the military base on the site. The museum includes 15 different aircraft types, including many genuine war relics, an Ilyushin IL-14 and other transport types. Open Wed-Sun, 10am-5pm.

Naval Aviation Museum

Vasco da Gama, Goa | www.goatourism.gov.in

A small museum in Goa, with a complete Indian Navy Lockheed Constellation aircraft on display amongst others. Open daily (except Monday) from 10am to 5pm.

INDONESIA

Capital: Jakarta

Overview

Indonesia is a vast network of islands stretching from Malaysia to Australia. Because of its layout, domestic air travel has always been a big part of life there. For many years the country was an outpost of older airliners still being flown, which attracted many enthusiasts. However, today the airlines operating here have largely updated their fleets to modern types.

Still worth visiting nevertheless, Indonesia's main airports are at the capital Jakarta, the tourist hub Bali, and the regional capitals Medan, Surabaya and Yogyakarta.

The largest airlines in Indonesia include national carrier Garuda and Citilink, plus Batik Air, Indonesia AirAsia, Lion Air, Sriwijaya Air and Wings Air.

Whilst it is not easy to venture into the remoter areas of the country, it is interesting to note the operations of Susi Air and other airlines which fly utility aircraft from some of the main hubs to tiny airstrips.

DENPASAR BALI NGURAH RAI INTERNATIONAL

DPS | WADD

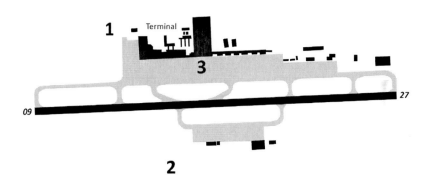

Denpasar Ngurah Rai International is the third busiest airport in Indonesia, and a busy tourist resort – particularly among Asians an Australians. The airport sees a good mix of exotic domestic aircraft and large international carriers on a daily basis, and is a hub for Garuda, Indonesia AirAsia, and Wings Air. Unfortunately, due to terrorist activity the airport became much more security conscious and increasingly more difficult to spot at; the best spotting location has now disappointingly been fenced off.

The airport spans a narrow strip of land between the ocean and an inlet to the east. It has a single runway, 09/27, which extends into the sea on reclaimed land.

Much of the northern side of the runway is taken up by the airliner parking stands and passenger terminal, while the south side has a smaller ramp for executive aircraft.

BASE FOR:
Garuda Indonesia
Indonesia AirAsia
Lion Air
Wings Air

↓

Spotting Locations

1. Kutra Beach

This was once an amazing position for photographing aircraft on the runway and taxiways close up. However, fences have now been erected on the breakwater which prevents you getting close and blocks any decent photography. Nevertheless, you can still see aircraft movements from this beach and read registrations.

2. Jimbaran

On the south side of the airport, the resort village of Jimbaran has a number of streets which lead to crash gates fronting the runway. It is easy to photograph aircraft through holes in the fence here, however security will often move spotters on from these locations. Jimbaran's beach also has opportunities to watch movements, but is not good for photography.

3. Terminal

On the departures level of the terminal, a narrow corridor can be found which has large windows overlooking the apron and runway. Photography is not ideal due to the glass, but it is the only worthwhile spot inside the building.

Spotting Hotel

H Sovereign Hotel

Jl. Raya Tuban No.2, Tuban, Kuta, Kabupaten Badung, Bali 80361, Indonesia | +62 361 301 5555
www.hsovereignhotels.com

At the eastern end of the airport, a couple of streets north of the runway 27 threshold. Aircraft arriving and departing can be seen from the rooftop pool area as well as some rooms facing towards the airport.

REGULAR:
Air Niugini
AirAsia
AirAsia X
Batik Air
Cathay Dragon
Cathay Pacific
Cebu Pacific
China Airlines
China Eastern
China Southern
Citilink
Emirates
EVA Air
Hong Kong Airlines
Jetstar Airways
Jetstar Asia Airways
KLM
Korean Air
Malaysia Airlines
Malindo Air
NAM Air
Philippine Airlines
Philippines AirAsia
Qantas
Qatar Airways
Royal Brunei
Scoot
SilkAir
Singapore Airlines
Sriwijaya Air
Thai AirAsia
Thai Airways
Thai Lion Air
TransNusa
Virgin Australia
XiamenAir

JAKARTA SOEKARNO-HATTA INTERNATIONAL

CGK | WIII

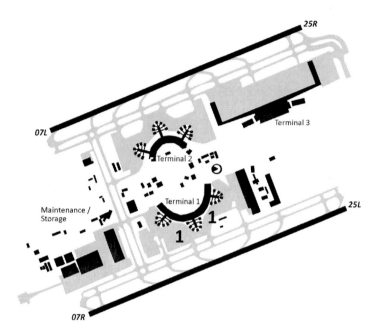

2
FM7
Hotel

Jakarta's main airport is the busiest in the country and has three terminals, with the two main ones having viewing galleries. It is the home base of Garuda Indonesia, Batik Air, Indonesia AirAsia and Lion Air.

The airport layout sees a pair of parallel runways, with the original Terminal 1 facing the southern runway, Terminal 2 facing the northern runway, and the brand-new Terminal 3 also facing this direction. The latter handles most of Garuda's flights, and it is anticipated that Terminal 4 will also be built in the near future.

BASE FOR:
Batik Air
Cardig Air
Citilink
Garuda Indonesia
Indonesia AirAsia
Lion Air
Nam Air
Sriwijaya Air

↓

Jakarta was somewhere enthusiasts flocked to see older classic jet and prop types, but these days are now gone save for some aircraft languishing in long term storage near the maintenance areas on the western portion of the airport.

There are a couple of good spotting hotels here, including one inside Terminal 2. You can travel freely between the three terminals using the monorail.

Spotting Locations

1. Terminal 1
This terminal has a number of so-called waving galleries along its length. Each is free to enter and offers a slightly different view to others. They offer good opportunities to photograph domestic aircraft, and some galleries look over the maintenance and storage areas. However, at the time of writing all but one of these galleries were closed and it is uncertain whether they will reopen in the future.

2. Spotting Hotels
(see later).

REGULAR:
Air China
Airfast Indonesia
All Nippon Airways
AirAsia
Asiana Airlines
Atlas Air
Aviastar
Cathay Pacific
Cebu Pacific
China Airlines
China Eastern
China Southern
Emirates
Ethiopian Airlines
Etihad Airways
EVA Air
FedEx Express
Flynas
Japan Airlines
Jet Asia Airways
Jestar Asia Airways
K-Mile Air
KLM
Korean Air
Malaysia Airlines
Malindo Air
My Indo Airlines
Oman Air
Philippine Airlines
Philippines AirAsia
Qantas
Qatar Airways
Raya Airways
Royal Brunei
Saudia
Scoot
Singapore Airlines
SriLankan Airlines
Thai Airways
Thai Lion Air
Tri-MG Intra Asia Airways
Trigana Air Service
Turkish Airlines
VietJet Air
Vietnam Airlines
XiamenAir

Spotting Hotels

Jakarta Airport Hotel

Terminal 2E, Soekarno-Hatta International Airport, Jakarta 19110 | +62 21 559 0008
www.jakartaairporthotel.com

This hotel is situated upstairs in Terminal 2 and all rooms look out over the gates and northern runway. The corridor leading to the rooms has windows looking towards the domestic side of the airport and maintenance areas.

FM7 Resort Hotel

Jl. Raya Perancis No. 67, Benda, Kec. Tgr, Banten 15125 | +62 21 559 11777
www.fm7hotel.com

The FM7 Resort Hotel is situated close to the end of Runway 25R, and one of the main benefits is the proximity of aircraft approaching this runway, which can be photographed quite easily. Although the hotel is only two stories high, rooms on the top floor can be found that have good views and are not too obstructed by the surrounding trees. Some rooms also have views across to runway 25L, but flight tracking websites or SBS are necessary to identify them as they disappear behind the buildings. A rooftop area also has views, but you may need to ask for it to be opened during the day.

SURABAYA JUANDA INTERNATIONAL

SUB | WARR

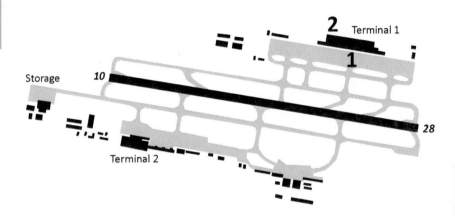

Indonesia's third busiest airport, located in central Java, around 500 miles east of Jakarta. It is a busy domestic hub and sees international service from some Asian carriers.

The airport has one runway and two terminals – one either side of the runway. Ultimately two more runways and a replacement terminal will be built as part of future plans.

To the east of Terminal 2, directly opposite Terminal 1, is a military base which often has transport aircraft present.

In the south-west corner of the airfield is a compound full of stored and retired airliners and the Merpati Training Centre. The aircraft can not easily be seen, and it helps if you're in a departing

BASE FOR:
Citilink
Garuda Indonesia
Indonesia AirAsia X
Lion Air
Sriwijaya Air

↓

or arriving aircraft to catch a view of all of them. You could also try to arrange a visit by contacting the centre.

Spotting Locations

1. Waving Gallery
A waving gallery is located in Terminal 1 for views across the parked aircraft and runway. Photography is possible, and the military area can be seen opposite.

2. Ibis Budget Hotel
(see later).

Spotting Hotel

Ibis Budget Hotel
Terminal 1, Jl. Ir. Juanda, Kec. Sidoarjo, 61253
+62 31 8688115 | www.ibis.com

Set within Terminal 1 at Surabaya. Its rooms are above the terminal, and any facing the airport has a ramp and runway view, so you can spot and usually photograph as you wish. The hotel is basic, but comfortable.

REGULAR:
AirAsia
Airfast Indonesia
Batik Air
Cathay Pacific
China Airlines
Jetstar Asia Airways
Malaysia Airlines
My Indo Airlines
NAM Air
Republic Express Airlines
Royal Brunei
Saudia
Scoot
SilkAir
Singapore Airlines
Trigana Air Service
Wings Air

OTHER AIRPORTS

Batam Hang Nadim International

BTH| WIDD

Batam incredibly has a 4,210m runway – the second longest in Asia. In fact, its proximity to Singapore means it has often acted as a diversion airport for Singapore Airlines and other carriers.

Day-to-day, this is a domestic airport with flights from Batik Air, Citilink, Garuda, Lion Air, Malindo Air, Sriwijaya, Susi Air and Wings Air. It handles around 6 million passengers per year, with a fairly small terminal on the north side of the runway. There are limited views of movements from inside.

Jakarta Halim Perdanakusuma

HLP | WIHH

Formerly the city's main airport until Soekarno Hatta opened in 1985, Halim is now a military base and is once again growing as a commercial airport, with domestic flights from Batik Air, Citilink, Pelita Air, Susi Air, TransNusa and Wings Air. Cargo operators are also common here.

Halim is also home to a maintenance base on its south side which often has aircraft in long-term storage. Although not as easy as it used to be, recent reports state it is still possible to arrange airside photography access at Halim. There are not many spotting locations outside the airport, and with the military presence it is not wise to act suspicious. Halim is located within the city, around 20 minutes' drive from the main airport.

Makassar Sultan Hasanuddin International

UPG | WAAA

A growing airport in eastern Indonesia, on the island of Sulawesi. It has a modern 2008-built passenger terminal alongside runway 03/21. The old, disused terminal and a military base are to its north, alongside runway 13/31. Expect to see mostly domestic flights from the main airlines, plus a selection of international and charter flights.

Sadly, there are no dedicated viewing areas, but passenger have good views from the departure lounge.

Medan Kualanamu International

KNO | WIMM

This brand-new airport opened in 2013, replacing the older Polonia International, which is now the Soewondo Air Force Base.

Kualanamu International is the fourth busiest in Indonesia, handling flights across the country as well as to international destinations in Asia. It has a single runway and terminal but is laid out ready for a parallel runway and more terminal facilities to be built in the future.

Views are possible from the departure lounge, but outside locations are difficult to come by.

Pondok Cabe Airport

PCB | WIHP

A small airport around 20 miles south of Jakarta which acts as a maintenance base for operators like Pelita Air Service, and is a base for the Indonesian National Police. It has limited domestic flights, but Garuda hopes to increase the number of operations here in the future.

Of interest to the spotter is the selection of airliners stored, derelict or visiting for maintenance. The best place to view these is from the road running the length of the runway on the opposite side to the terminal, where aircraft can be seen through the fence.

Yogyakarta Adisutjipto International

JOG | WAHH

Another busy airport on the island of Java, Yogyakarta is primarily a domestic facility with some limited international services. Citilink and Lion Air are the busiest operators.

The airport has a single runway and two small terminals on the north side. There are no official viewing areas, but aircraft can

The nearby Dirgantara Mandala Air Force Museum is worth visiting. From there, any aircraft arriving from the west pass almost directly overhead.

MUSEUMS

Dirgantara Mandala Air Force Museum

Kompleks Landasan Udara Adisucipto, Jl. Kolonel Sugiono, Banguntapan, Yogyakarta, Bantul, Daerah Istimewa Yogyakarta 55282, Indonesia | +62 274 564 466

A museum of the Indonesian Air Force just to the west of Yogyakarta Airport. It houses an interesting collection of military aircraft, including some transport types like the Douglas DC-3. Open daily except Monday from 8am-1pm (12pm on Friday and Saturday).

Satriamandala Museum

Jl. Gatot Subroto No.16, RT.6/RW.1, Kuningan Bar., Mampang Prpt., Kota Jakarta Selatan, Daerah Khusus Ibukota Jakarta 12710, Indonesia

Located in south Jakarta, near the Four Seasons Hotel, this is a museum of the Indonesian armed forces with various artefacts, including a number of aircraft such as the Douglas DC-3 and B-25 Mitchell. Open daily from 7am-3pm (from 9am on Sunday).

JAPAN

Capital: Tokyo

Overview

Spotting in Japan can be a delight for enthusiasts. It is a country where provisions are made, with most airports featuring at least one public viewing area, usually on top of the terminal with great views.

It is also a country with a heavy emphasis on air transport. Traditionally the country's two main airlines, All Nippon Airways and Japan Airlines, would use large aircraft on domestic trunk routes, and smaller ones on a complex network of thinner routes. This is still the case.

Then there are the major hubs, like Tokyo's two airports, plus those at Osaka, Nagoya, Sapporo and Fukuoka. These are busy airports, often with a good selection of international carriers to keep things interesting.

Language barriers can make life difficult in Japan for western visitors, but in all the major cities English speakers can be found, and many signs also have English translations on them particularly in airports, tourist areas and rail stations.

CHUBU CENTRAIR INTERNATIONAL

NGO | RJGG

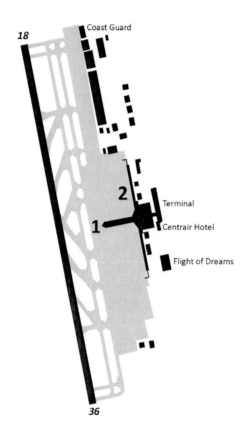

Chubu Centrair is one of Japan's newest airports built, like several others in Japan, on an artificial island close to the coast near Nagoya. It was opened in February 2005 to replace the older airport at Nagoya; its name is a play on its location, serving the heavily populated central region of Japan. It is around 180 miles from Tokyo.

BASE FOR:
All Nippon Airways
Jetstar Japan
AirAsia Japan

↓

Because of its newness, Centrair is a very modern airport with amenities to attract discerning travellers.

It has a single, large terminal with one central pier, and two piers stretching in either direction away from the central building. In front is the airport's only runway, 18/36, and to the north is one of Japan's largest cargo terminals.

The Coast Guard also base aircraft at this airport, with facilities at the northern end of the site.

Enthusiasts will want to visit the brand new Flight of Dreams centre at the airport, which features one of the prototype Boeing 787 Dreamliner aircraft, ZA001, donated by the manufacturer.

Spotting Locations

1. Observation Deck
By far the easiest and best location for spotting at Chubu, the official Observation Deck runs along the top of the central pier atop the terminal with good views of the gates and runway. This is a large, popular deck which is open from 7am-9pm, free of charge. It has tall wire fencing running along its length, but it is still possible to poke a camera through to take photographs.

2. Domestic Terminal Gate Area
If the weather isn't good enough to be outside, you can shelter in the domestic gate area of the terminal where large windows offer plenty of views of the aircraft and runway beyond. You can't see the international gates from here, but aircraft will be visible when using the runway.

REGULAR:
AirBridgeCargo
Air Busan
Air China
Air Do
Asiana Airlines
Cathay Pacific
Cebu Pacific
China Airlines
China Eastern
China Southern
Delta
DHL Aviation
Etihad Airways
Finnair
HK Express
Ibex Airlines
Japan Airlines
Japan Transocean Air
Jeju Air
Juneyao Airlines
Korean Air
Lufthansa
National Airlines
Nippon Cargo
Philippine Airlines
Singapore Airlines
Skymark Airlines
Solaseed Air
Spring Airlines
StarFlyer
Thai Airways
Tigerair Taiwan
Transmile Air Services
ULS Cargo
United Airlines
Vietnam Airlines

Spotting Hotel

Centrair Hotel
1 Chrome-1 Centrair, Tokoname | +81 569 38 1111 | www.centrairhotel.jp

The closest hotel to the airport terminal. It is a tall hotel, and upper rooms facing the airport have views of movements on the runway and domestic side of the terminal.

Public Transport

The airport is linked via train to Meitetsu-Nagoya Station, which is connected to the Shinkansen high-speed network. Ferries also connect the passenger terminal with the mainland.

FUKUOKA AIRPORT

FUK | RJFF

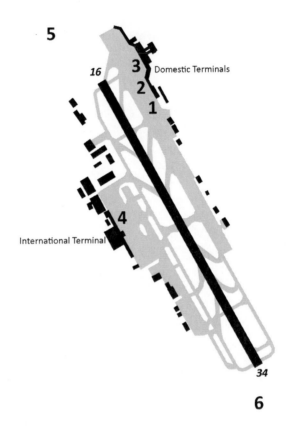

Fukuoka Airport handles a mix of domestic and intra-Asian flights from a variety of airlines. It is the fourth busiest airport in Japan and has little room to expand owing to the city encroaching on all sides.

There are three domestic passenger terminals–1, 2 and 3–on the northern side of the single runway, and an International Terminal on the opposite side. A Coast Guard station is situated alongside the International Terminal.

As with most Japanese airports, enthusiasts are catered for by observation decks on all terminals.

REGULAR:
Air Busan
Air China
Air Macau
Air Seoul
All Nippon Airways
Amakusa Airlines
ANA Wings
Asiana Airlines
Cathay Dragon
Cebu Pacific
China Airlines

↓

Spotting Locations

1. Domestic Terminal 1 Observation Deck

All three domestic terminals have their own observation deck. The one at Terminal 1 is outdoor and accessed from floor 2F in the departures area. It is free of charge and open from 7am to 8pm. This is a good all-round location for aircraft using the runway and domestic terminals. Large fences front the deck, which can hinder photography but is usually acceptable.

2. Domestic Terminal 1 Observation Room

Accessed via a spiral staircase from floor 3F, Terminal 1's alternative observation area is indoors and fronted by glass windows. This can sometimes hinder photography, but the views are great and it's a nice warm place to spot in harsh weather. Free of charge, and open 7am to 8pm.

3. Domestic Terminal 2 Observation Deck

You can access this rooftop deck from floor 3F near the games room. A slightly more spacious area to spot, which has glass windows instead of fences. The glass is usually clean enough to take photographs through. Views are of the southern end of the domestic terminal and the runway. You can see across to the International Terminal too. Free of charge, and open from 7am to 9.30pm.

4. International Terminal Observation Decks

There are two observation decks atop the International Terminal and accessed from either end of the building. These have views over the international gates, runway, and across to the domestic terminals. The decks are surrounded by glass, so photographs are not always perfect. Free of charge and open from 7am to 8pm.

5. Runway 16

There are a few points around the perimeter fence close to the end of Runway 16. From these you can take good unobstructed views of aircraft landing on this runway, and you'll often find other spotters here. You can see some movements

China Eastern
China Southern
China United
Delta
Eastar Jet
EVA Air
Finnair
Fuji Dream Airlines
HK Express
Ibex Airlines
Japan Airlines
J-Air
Japan Air Commuter
Japan Transocean Air
Jeju Air
Jetstar Japan
Jin Air
Korean Air
Oriental Air Bridge
Peach
Philippine Airlines
Skymark Airlines
Singapore Airlines
StarFlyer
T'way Airlines
Thai Airways
Tigerair Taiwan
United Airlines
Vanilla Air
Vietnam Airlines

on the ground through the fence. You can reach these points by walking alongside the fence from Terminal 2 for around 15 minutes.

6. Runway 34

Two spots near the end of this runway are great for photographs of aircraft landing and lining up for departure. The first is a mound next to a small road (where you can park). Take bus 43 from the domestic terminal and get off at Tsukiguma. This is good on the morning.

The second spot is a footbridge on the other side of the runway which is good on the afternoon for photography. The gas station nearby is useful for supplies.

OKINAWA NAHA

OKA | ROAH

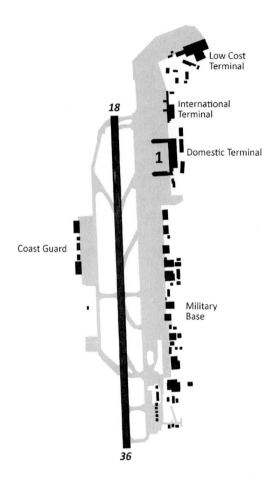

Low Cost
Terminal

18

International
Terminal

1 Domestic Terminal

Coast Guard

Military
Base

36

A single runway airport which is a joint military base. Okinawa is Japan's seventh-busiest and serves mainly domestic flights, with a mix of international services to the likes of China, Hong Kong and Taiwan.

The terminals and cargo complex are in the north-east corner of the airport. To the south is the expansive JASDF base, whilst on the western side of the runway is a Coast Guard station. It makes for an interesting mix of movements.

BASE FOR:
Japan Transocean Air
Peach
Ryuku Air Commuter

↓

A second parallel runway is currently being built to the west on reclaimed land, due to open in 2020.

Spotting Locations

1. Terminal Observation Decks
There are two observation decks on top of the Domestic Terminal from which all movements can be seen, including anything operating from the military side. There is a fee to enter.

REGULAR:
Air China
All Nippon Airways
ANA Wings
Beijing Capital Airlines
Cathay Dragon
China Airlines
China Eastern
Eastar Jet
EVA Air
Hong Kong Airlines
Japan Airlines
Jeju Air
Jetstar Asia
Jetstar Japan
Jin Air
Juneyao Airlines
Korean Air
Mandarin Airlines
SilkAir
Skymark Airlines
Solaseed Air
T'way Airlines
Tigerair Taiwan
Vanilla Air

OSAKA ITAMI

ITM | RJOO

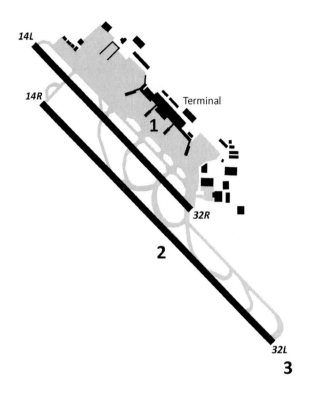

The original airport for Osaka, Itami is now relegated to domestic operations, with international services flown out of Kansai International to the south of the city.

Itami is surrounded on all sides by the city, and it is one of the busiest in Japan for aircraft movements. A perfect place to catch up on the domestic airline fleets, here you will primarily see the country's two main operators–Japan Airlines and All Nippon Airways (and their feeder carriers) operating throughout the country with various aircraft types from commuter turboprops to widebodies.

BASE FOR:
All Nippon Airways
Japan Airlines

REGULAR:
Amakusa Airlines

There are two parallel runways at the airport. The terminal building, which is split into two section, plus the parking apron, are on the northern side.

Spotting Locations

1. Observation Deck
The airport's observation deck is located on top of the terminal building and overlooks the runways and many of the gates. Photography is good from here, although air bridges can get in the way of closer shots. The observation deck is open from 8am-10pm and is free of charge. You can access it on the 3rd floor.

2. Itami Sky Park
Situated on the opposite side of the airport, the Sky Park is another viewing area provided for spotters. This garden-like structure has various levels allowing photography above the fence of aircraft on the main 14R/32L runway. The Sky Park extends for quite a distance along the airport perimeter. It is an excellent spot in good weather, and free to use. There are nearby convenience stores for supplies. You can take a bus 25 from the terminal every 30 minutes (alight after passing the tunnel under the runway).

3. Runway 32L
A track runs by the end of runway 32L which is a good place to photograph aircraft just before touchdown and whilst on the runway. It is possible to drive along the track, which links two city roads. Be careful not to cause an obstruction.

OSAKA KANSAI INTERNATIONAL

KIX | RJBB

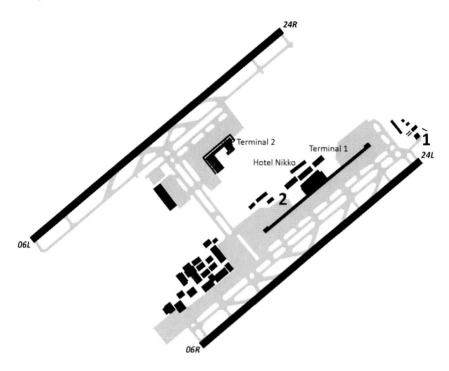

Kansai Airport replaced Itami as the main international gateway to Osaka in 1994. Itami remains open as a domestic airport, however Kansai is now the larger and busier gateway. It was constructed on a man-made island in Osaka Bay and later expanded with a second runway. A second terminal opened in 2012 for the use of low-cost operators, and it is anticipated that a third runway will also be built.

Kansai is a major cargo centre – one of the busiest freight airports in the world. Freighters of all the world's major cargo airlines are a daily sight, using facilities to the south-west of the passenger terminals.

BASE FOR:
All Nippon Airways
FedEx Express
Japan Airlines
Jetstar Japan
Nippon Cargo Airlines
Peach

REGULAR:
Air Busan
Air Canada
Air China
Air France
Air Hong Kong
Air India
Air Macau
Air New Zealand
Air Seoul
AirAsia X

↓

All major Japanese and Asian airlines fly to Kansai, as well as a number of low-cost carriers and airlines from Europe, North America and the Middle East.

Spotting Locations

1. Sky View Observation Hall
The official spotting location at Kansai is an elevated platform at the eastern end of the airport, close to the threshold of runway 24L. It has excellent views over this runway and the terminal gates, so you won't miss any aircraft or registrations. Photography is also good, with the classic view of aircraft passing over the road bridge possible. The Observation Hall is free and open 8am-10pm (10pm at weekends). You can reach it via the bus from the terminal (Nankai bus stop), signposted to the Observation Hall.

2. Outside Terminal 1
At departures level of Terminal 1, you can walk outside in either direction and come to positions where views of the apron, taxiways and parked aircraft are possible.

Spotting Hotel

Hotel Nikko Kansai Airport
Kansai Airport, Osaka 549-0001 | +81 455 1111
www.nikkokix.com

This hotel is linked to the terminal and railway station. Rooms on the top floor facing the airport have views of the taxiway, runways and part of the terminal.

Public Transport

Various rail routes link Kansai Airport to locations on the mainland, including downtown Osaka and its public transport network, plus onward connections around the country. Bus services also connect the airport to the city.

Aircalin
Asiana Airlines
Beijing Capital Airlines
Cathay Pacific
Cebu Pacific
China Airlines
China Cargo Airlines
China Eastern
China Postal Airlines
China Southern
Delta
Eastar Jet
EgyptAir
Emirates
EVA Air
Finnair
Garuda Indonesia
Hawaiian Airlines
Hong Kong Airlines
HK Express
Japan Transocean Air
Jeju Air
Jetstar Airways
Jetstar Asia
Jetstar Pacific
Jin Air
Juneyao Airlines
KLM
Korean Air
Lufthansa
Malaysia Airlines
Okay Airways
Philippine Airlines
Polar Air Cargo
Qantas
S7 Airlines
Scoot
Shanghai Airlines
Shandong Airlines
Sichuan Airlines
Singapore Airlines
Spring Airlines
StarFlyer
Thai AirAsia X
Thai Airways
Tianjin Airlines
Tigerair Taiwan
T'way Airlines
United Airlines
UPS Airlines
Vanilla Air
Vietjet Air
Vietnam Airlines
XiamenAir
Yakutia Airlines

SAPPORO NEW CHITOSE

CTS | RJCC

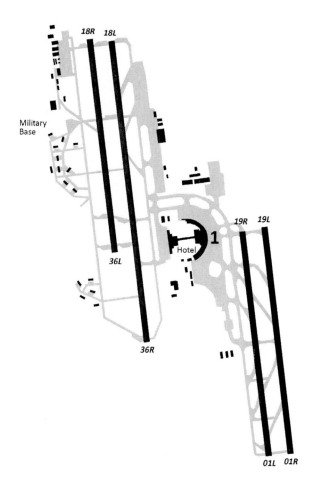

The largest airport on the northern island of Hokkaido. New Chitose is a joint civil-military airport, which is home to a JASDAF squadron of F-15's, as well as the government transport aircraft.

The civilian airport operates from the eastern side of the site, with two parallel runways and a semi-circular domestic terminal building. The small international terminal is behind, on the western side.

REGULAR:
AirAsia Japan
AirAsia X
Air Busan
Air China
Air Do
Air Seoul
All Nippon Airways
ANA Wings

↓

To the west you'll find the military side, with its own pair of parallel runways and facilities. On occasion aircraft from either side will use the other's runways.

The airport sees a good mix of international and domestic scheduled services, and in particular is good for the smaller regional aircraft of the various Japanese airlines.

Spotting Locations

1. Terminal Observation Areas
There is an outdoor observation area on the fourth floor of the domestic terminal, open 9am to 5pm in the summer, but closed in winter. Indoors, another observation hall is available year-round.

Spotting Hotel

Air Terminal Hotel
New Chitose Airport | +81 123 45 6677
www.air-terminal-hotel.jp

Situated at the southern end of the passenger terminal. Directions are difficult, but once you find the place it is comfortable and perfect for a layover. One side of the hotel has rooms facing the parking apron and runways beyond, so is the best hotel option at the airport.

Asia Atlantic Airlines
Asiana Airlines
Aurora
Cathay Pacific
China Airlines
China Eastern
China Southern
Eastar Jet
EVA Air
Fuji Dream Airlines
Hainan Airlines
Hong Kong Airlines
Japan Airlines
J-Air
Jeju Air
Jetstar Japan
Jin Air
Juneyao Airlines
Korean Air
Peach
Philippine Airlines
Scoot
Singapore Airlines
Skymark Airlines
T'way Airlines
Thai AirAsia X
Thai Airways
Tianjin Airlines
Vanilla Air

TOKYO HANEDA INTERNATIONAL

HND | RJTT

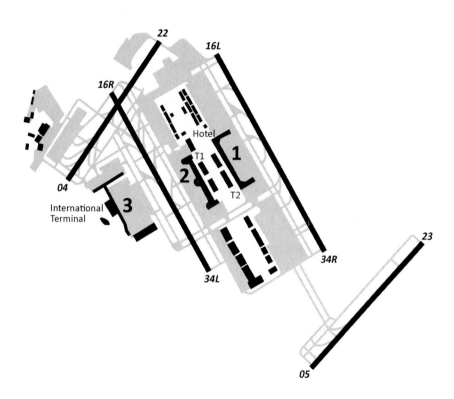

Haneda is one of the best airports to spot at in Japan, and is now the fourth-busiest airport in the world. It provides observation decks on all terminals, including the newer International Terminal, giving you plenty of space to observe the vast number of aircraft passing through the airport.

It has undergone a number of expansions and improvements over the past decade, including the new terminal and a fourth runway opened in 2010. Many more international flights now also fly from Haneda, where Narita previously had a monopoly on this. Combined with the large number of domestic and intra-Asian

BASE FOR:
Air Do
All Nippon Airways
Japan Airlines
Skymark Airlines
Solaseed Air
StarFlyer

↓

flights, it makes Haneda a very busy airport indeed – so much so that it can be difficult to cover everything given the different aspects faced by each viewing deck. Spotters must move about to catch as much as possible, using the position of the sun to determine the best place to be for photographs.

The layout of Haneda is quite complicated. Two pairs of parallel runways run in two different directions, with the most recent built on reclaimed land in the bay. The domestic terminals sit centrally, between the 16/34 runways, whilst the ANA and JAL maintenance hangars are to their south.

Over on the south-west side of the airport is the International Terminal, whilst in the north-west corner are areas used by executive aircraft and the Coast Guard.

Spotting Locations

1. Terminal 1 Observation Deck
Terminal 1's observation deck overlooks that terminal and the new International Terminal across runway 16R/34L. You will see JAL and its associate airlines here. It is free to enter, and open from 6.30am to 10pm daily. The deck is accessed from the centre of the building via lift or escalator. Although there are tall fences around the deck, enlarged holes are provided for sticking camera lenses through. Photography is best in the morning.

2. Terminal 2 Observation Deck
On the opposite side to the Terminal 1 deck, this one overlooks runway 16L/34R. It is also open from 6.30am to 10pm daily, and free of charge. This deck covers ANA and its associates, plus Air Do and Solaseed. It is better for photography from mid-morning onwards, but fewer movements are seen overall.

REGULAR:
AirAsia X
Air Canada
Air China
Air France
Air Incheon
Air New Zealand
American Airlines
Asiana Airlines
British Airways
Cathay Dragon
Cathay Pacific
China Airlines
China Eastern
China Southern
Delta
Emirates
EVA Air
Garuda Indonesia
Hainan Airlines
Hawaiian Airlines
HK Express
Hong Kong Airlines Cargo
Juneyao Airlines
Korean Air
Lufthansa
Okay Airways
Peach
Philippine Airlines
Qantas
Qatar Airways
Shanghai Airlines
Singapore Airlines
Spring Airlines
Thai Airways
Tianjin Airlines
Tigerair Taiwan
United Airlines
Vietnam Airlines

3. International Terminal Observation Deck

This newer terminal also has a free deck on top, which is open the same times and is free of charge. It looks over the international gates, runway 16R/34L and across to Terminal 1. Light is best from mid-morning, but again you'll have to grapple with the high fence and limited holes to stick a lens through. You'll see most movements from here.

Spotting Hotel

Haneda Excel Hotel Tokyo

3-4-2 Hanedakuko Ota, 144-0041 Tokyo | +81 3 5756 6000
www.tokyuhotelsjapan.com/en/

Linked to Terminal 2, this hotel offers some of the best views at the airport if you get the right room. Ask for a higher floor room facing the airport. It is quite expensive to stay at this hotel, but the location is superb. The observation decks at the terminals are only a short walk away.

Public Transport

The Access Express train service linked Haneda with Narita direct in around 1.5 hours.

You can take the local Keikyu train or Tokyo Monorail to reach downtown Tokyo from stations at Haneda Airport.

TOKYO NARITA INTERNATIONAL

NRT | RJAA

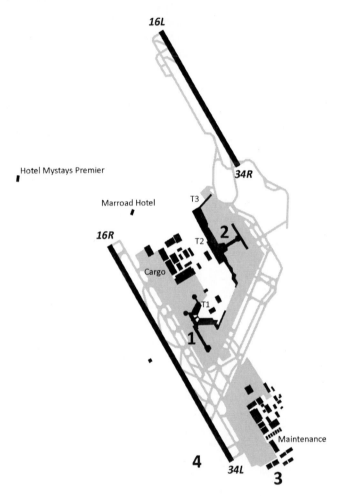

Narita is Japan's second busiest airport, situated some 60 miles north of Tokyo. Primarily an international gateway, much of this traffic has now transferred back to Haneda, with plans for Narita to become more of a low-cost airport. Nevertheless, today it remains a busy place with airlines from all over the world flying in.

BASE FOR:
All Nippon Airways
Japan Airlines
Jetstar Japan
Nippon Cargo
Peach
Vanilla Air

↓

Narita has three passenger terminals in the central area and a large cargo terminal to the north. To the south, Japan Airlines handle maintenance of their fleet.

The full length of the newer runway 16L/34R was never realised due to conflicts with local land owners. Future plans will see this runway extended to full length, and a third runway also built to the east.

Spotting Locations

1. Terminal 1 Observation Deck
The largest of the official spotting locations at Narita. It is located atop Terminal 1 and is free to enter. It has views over the gates, taxiways and the main runway, and photography is good on a morning (through holes in the fence). You will see most international and cargo flights from this deck. It is accessed from level 4F inside the terminal, and open from 7am to 9pm. There is no WiFi at this deck.

2. Terminal 2 Observation Decks
Terminal 2 has two observation decks–one either side of the pier. They are both free to enter, and open from 7am to 9pm, with WiFi. The southern deck has better views of the taxiways, but the northern one has views of some gates that are not visible to the other. You will see the low-cost carriers better from Terminal 2. Photography is possible through enlarged holes in the fence, and light is best in the afternoon.

3. Museum of Aeronautical Sciences/Runway 34L
Whilst the Aviation Museum is worth a visit in its own right, it also features an observation deck which is good for views of aircraft approaching runway 34L and on the taxiways linking it. It makes for good photographs. If you don't have a car, take bus from Terminal 1 stop No. 30.

From the museum you can walk around the southern end of Runway 34L to Hikoki-no Oka

REGULAR:
Aeroflot
Aeromexico
AirBridgeCargo
Air Busan
Air Canada
Air China
Air France
Air Hong Kong
Air Incheon
Air India
Air Macau
Air New Zealand
Air Niugini
Air Seoul
Air Tahiti Nui
Aircalin
Alitalia
American Airlines
Asiana Airlines
Atlas Air
Austrian Airlines
British Airways
Cargolux
Cathay Pacific
Cebu Pacific
Centurion Air Cargo
China Airlines
China Cargo Airlines
China Eastern
China Southern
Delta
Eastar Jet
EgyptAir
Emirates
Ethiopian Airlines
Etihad Airways
EVA Air
FedEx Express
Fiji Airways
Finnair
Garuda Indonesia
Hainan Airlines
Hawaiian Airlines
Hong Kong Airlines
HK Express
Iberia
Indonesia AirAsia X
Jeju Air
Jet Asia Airways
Jetstar Airways
Jin Air

↓

Park where photography on an afternoon is perfect if aircraft are landing in this direction.

4. Sakura no Yama Park

Situated near the end of runway 16R and ideal if aircraft are landing on this runway. Good for photographs, although the perimeter fence can sometimes get in the way. You also have good views over the western side of the airport. Many people come here, although you'll need a car (follow Route 44 southeast from the airport). It is a 15-minute walk from the Marroad Hotel.

Spotting Hotels

Marroad International Hotel

763-1 Komaino, Narita-shi, Chiba 286-0121
+81 476 30 2222 | www.marroad.jp/narita/

Situated close to the threshold of runway 16R. If you ask for a room facing the airport, you will have views of this runway, the cargo apron and part of Terminal 1. Photographs are possible, and most movements can be logged. The hotel's top-floor restaurant also has good views. Reasonably priced, with a free shuttle to the airport.

Hotel Mystays Premier Narita

31 Oyama, Narita-shi, Chiba 286-0131
+81 476 33 0133 | www.tokyuhotelsjapan.com/en/

Again, situated close to runway 16R and airport facing rooms have views of most movements. Photography is not good from here, however. A little more expensive than the Marroad, but worth it for seeing more movements and the arrivals screens in the lobby. Also has a free shuttle.

KLM
Korean Air
LOT Polish Airlines
Malaysia Airlines
Mandarin Airlines
MIAT Mongolian
NokScoot
Pakistan International
Philippine Airlines
Polar Air Cargo
Qantas
Qatar Airways
S7 Airlines
Scandinavian Airlines
Scoot
Shenzhen Airlines
Sichuan Airlines
Singapore Airlines
Southern Air
Spring Airlines
SriLankan Airlines
Swiss International
Thai AirAsia X
Thai Airways
Tigerair Taiwan
Turkish Airlines
T'way Airlines
Uni-Top Airlines
United Airlines
UPS Airlines
Uzbekistan Airways
Vietnam Airlines
XiamenAir
Yakutia Airlines
Yanda Airlines

OTHER AIRPORTS

Hiroshima Airport

HIJ | RJOA

Hiroshima has a single terminal building north of the runway, split into domestic and international sections. It sees domestic flights from all of the main airlines, plus international links by the likes of Air China, Air Seoul, China Airlines, China Eastern, HK Express and SilkAir.

There is a viewing deck along the front of the terminal which is perfect for spotting, but faces south which makes photography difficult.

Ibaraki Airport / Hyakuri Air Base

IBR | RJAH

Ibaraki Airport shares its parallel 03/21 runways with the Hyakuri JASDF Air Base, situated on the eastern side. The small passenger terminal is on the western side, with flights by Eastar Jet, Fuji Dream, Skymark Airlines, Spring Airlines and Tigerair Taiwan.

There is an observation deck on the second floor of the terminal, with views of aircraft movements on the runways (including those from the air base). The Airport Park outside the terminal has two preserved F-4 Phantom jets.

Kagoshima Airport

KOJ | RJFK

Located at the southern tip of Japan on Kyushu. Kagoshima is a busy domestic hub with international links to China, Hong Kong and South Korea. There is a viewing area on top of the terminal building which is great for photography on an afternoon. You will see all movements from here.

Kobe Airport

UKB | RJOA

Kobe is a smaller regional airport, with services by ANA, Air Do, Ibex Airlines, Solaseed and Skymark. It is situated offshore, with a single runway, and an observation deck on the fourth floor.

Kumamoto Airport

KMJ | RJFT

A single runway airport served by domestic and some international carriers. Kumamoto is also home to an Army National Guard base, with helicopters usually present.

There is an observation deck on the third floor of the domestic side of the airport. Look out also for a preserved NAMC YS-11 airliner outside the terminal.

Miyazaki Airport

KMI | RJFM

A modest regional airport with some international routes provided by Asiana Airlines, China Airlines, Eastar Jet and Hong Kong Airlines, among the regular domestic carriers. An observation deck atop the terminal has a preserved Beech King Air as an added attraction, as well as views of aircraft movements.

Nagasaki Airport

NGS | RJFU

Another of Japan's 'island airports', built off shore from the city and linked via a road bridge.

Nagasaki Airport has a single runway and a modest passenger terminal and a useful observation deck atop. Movements include All Nippon, Japan Airlines, Jetstar Japan, Peach, Skymark and Solaseed Air.

Just across the bridge on the mainland is Omura Air Base, which is used by JASDF for helicopter operations.

Nagoya Komaki

NKM | RJNA

Nagoya's original airport is in the north of the city is now known as Nagoya Airfield. It is home to Fuji Dream Airways and has a military air base, but little else of note. The airport has a single runway. The passenger terminal has an observation deck which is fine for watching movements.

Sendai Airport

SDJ | RJSS

Sendai has a main east-west runway, with a shorter strip crossing to the south and used mostly by general aviation traffic.

The passenger terminal is at the eastern end of the airport. Despite its modern design, it still finds space for a small observation deck overlooking the gates and main runway, known as the "Smile Terrace". It is open from 6.45am to 8pm daily.

At the western end of the main runway you'll find Sendaikukorinku Park where locals and enthusiasts gather to watch aircraft at close quarters. It's great for photography of aircraft on the runway and taxiway. There is a large car park, or it takes an hour to walk from the terminal.

MUSEUMS

Kakamigahara Aerospace Museum

5-1 Shimogiri-cho, Kakamigahara 504-0924 | +81 583 86 8500

An interesting collection of some 25 aircraft just south of the Gifu Airbase in Nagoya. Exhibits include a NAMC YS-11 and Grumman Albatross. Served by buses from central Nagoya. Open daily except Tuesday from 9.30am-4.30pm (5pm in summer).

Misawa Aviation and Science Museum

Kitayama 158, Misawa City, Aomori 033-022 | www.kokukagaku.jp

A mostly military museum located alongside Misawa Air Base in the region of Aomori. As well as the aircraft exhibits, which include a NAMC YS-11, you have good views of the air base's movements from the observation deck. Open daily 9am-5pm.

Museum of Aeronautical Sciences

111-3 Higashisanrizuka, Narita 288-0112 | +81 479 78 0557 | www.aeromuseum.or.jp

Located close to the end of runway 34L at Tokyo Narita Airport, with its own observation deck. This museum has a nice little collection of civil aircraft and helicopters. The largest preserved type is a NAMC YS-11 airliner and a Boeing 747 nose section. The museum is open 10am-5pm Tuesday-Sunday (daily in January, May and August), with a 500 yen entrance fee.

Shuttle buses depart from Terminal 1 (first floor, stop No. 30) and Terminal 2 (third floor, stop No. 2) for the museum. The trip takes 15 minutes and costs 200 yen. There are only four buses per day. Alternatively, a taxi ride from the airport costs about 1600 yen.

Tokorozawa Aviation Museum

359-0042 Saitama Prefecture, Tokorozawa, Namiki, 1-13

An aviation museum of some 30 exhibits on the historic site of Japan's first airfield, with some remnants still visible. The museum's collection is varied, with many early and military types and some civilian types like the Curtiss Commando and NAMC YS-11. The museum is around 30km north east of central Tokyo, linked to the local rail network. Open Tuesday-Sunday, 9.30am-5pm.

LAOS

Capital: Vientiane

Overview

Like Cambodia, Laos is another Asian country which is not as developed as some of its neighbours and can therefore make an interesting diversion to find some unusual aircraft for the log book. It is, however, a country where spotting may not be accepted, and discretion is advised – especially where airports share facilities with military users.

Vientiane is the main gateway, served in particular by Chinese and Thai airlines as well as domestic operators.

PRINCIPAL AIRPORTS

VIENTIANE WATTAY INTERNATIONAL

VTE | VLVT

Wattay International sits close to the border with Thailand, and is the main international airport of Laos.

The airport has a single runway, 13/31, and a small collection of terminal and administration buildings alongside a long parking apron.

The civil facilities are shared by a Lao Air Force base, slightly hidden away to the south of the terminals. Another apron in the north-east corner of the airport is often used for long-term aircraft parking, as well as military aircraft. Look out for a preserved Antonov An-2 at the base entrance.

Spotting is possible from upstairs in the domestic terminal, where views of movements and airliners parked on the ramp are good. Photography is also possible, but be discrete.

BASE FOR:
Lao Air
Lao Airlines

REGULAR:
AirAsia
Air Busan
Bangkok Airways
China Eastern
China Southern
Hainan Airlines
Jeju Air
Jin Air
Lao Skyway
Sichuan Airlines
T'way Airlines
Thai AirAsia
Thai Airways
Thai Smile
Vietnam Airlines

OTHER AIRPORTS

Luang Prabang International

LPQ | VLLB

The country's second busiest airport, with a single runway and recently upgraded facilities. It is a hub for Lao Airlines and served by carriers from neighbouring countries such as AirAsia, China Eastern, Hainan, SilkAir, Thai Smile and Vietnam Airlines among others. The small parking apron is partially visible from outside the terminal, and also through the windows once past security.

On the northern side of the runway, the main road has various side roads leading off through residential areas. Some of these end at the fence with views over the runway.

Keep away from the military apron on the west side.

MACAU

Capital: Macau

CHINA

MACAU

Overview

An autonomous part of China in the Pearl River Delta, close to Hong Kong. Macau is an important leisure destination – the "Las Vegas of Asia" – with its own based airline. As well as Hong Kong, Macau is a short distance from the Chinese cities of Guangzhou and Shenzhen.

MACAU INTERNATIONAL

MFM | VMMC

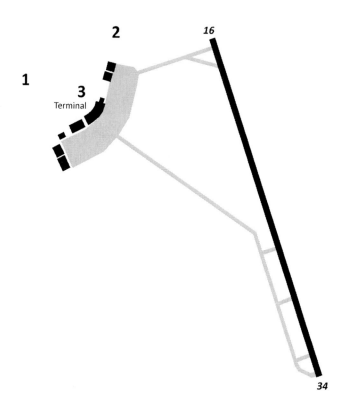

Macau International is located on the eastern edge of the region, with its single runway 16/34 built on reclaimed land in the sea. Most arrivals are from the south.

The single, fairly small, terminal and parking apron are underneath the Tam Hill Garden which overlooks the airport.

Movements are dominated by based Air Macau and its narrow body Airbus fleets. Other carriers from across the Far East and China all visit, but

BASE FOR:
Air Macau

REGULAR:
AirAsia
Air Busan
Air China
Bassaka Air
Beijing Capital
Cambodia Angkor Air

↓

there are few long-haul links or cargo services. Because of its reputation as a gambling centre, Macau Airport also sees plenty of executive movements. It is not, however, a particularly busy airport compared to many others in China.

Cebu Pacific
China Eastern
EVA Air
Hainan Airlines
Jeju Air
Jin Air
Juneyao Airlines
JC International
Lanmei Airlines
MASKargo
Philippine Airlines
Scoot
Shenzhen Airlines
Siam Air
Spring Airlines
Thai AirAsia
Tigerair Taiwan
T'way Airlines
XiamenAir

Spotting Locations

1. Tam Hill Garden
Overlooking the airport, this is a good place to watch movements around the terminal from a public place. It is too distant for photography, and the runway is a little far off.

2. Taipa Ferry Terminal
Just to the north of the airport is this ferry terminal which links Macau with Hong Kong and other areas (a useful way of travelling between the two airports). From here you have some views of the airport and movements on the taxiway. There is also a helipad on top of the building.

3. Golden Crown Hotel
(see later).

Spotting Hotel

Golden Crown China Hotel
Macau Airport | +853 2885 1166 | www.htlchina.com.mo

A very tall hotel situated outside the terminal at Macau Airport. Higher rooms have a grandstand view over the action, with 1701-1719, 1801-1813, 1901-1913 and 2001-2013 the best. You can see aircraft coming to and from the terminal and movements on the distant runway.

MALAYSIA

Capital: Kuala Lumpur

Overview

Malaysia is a popular destination for spotters, with a good mix of aircraft to see and some useful spotting locations.

Kuala Lumpur's main airport is the natural draw and offers good opportunities. The older airport in the city, once known as Subang, is also an interesting diversion when visiting the area.

Most of the other airports in the country are used for domestic flights with some regional links to nearby countries. You may find some interesting aircraft not seen in Kuala Lumpur, however.

The hobby is generally understood and tolerated in Malaysia as long as the usual precautions and common sense are observed. However, venturing too close to airport fences usually attracts attention from security, so it's best to stay to designated areas.

PRINCIPAL AIRPORTS

KOTA KINABALU INTERNATIONAL

BKI | WBKK

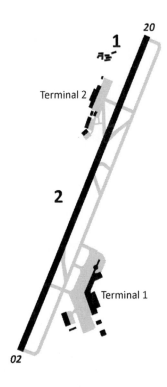

The principal airport in Salah, the remotest part of Malaysia. It is the country's busiest after Kuala Lumpur International, serving over 8 million passengers and airlines across the Far East.

The airport has a single runway, 02/20, and a single terminal. The former Terminal 2 on the opposite side of the runway is used for executive flights.

Terminal 1 has good views over the runway one airside.

BASE FOR:
AirAsia
Malaysia Airlines
MASWings

↓

Spotting Locations

1. Runway Café

Close to the runway 20 threshold at the northern end of the airport is the Runway Café which serves food and drink, and has views of aircraft approaching, including from its car park.

2. Jalan Johor

From the former Terminal 2, where you may see some aircraft parked on its apron, continue south past the police helicopter hangar along Jalan Johor. Eventually it passes a spot with good views across the runway towards Terminal 1, and local spotters often come here. It can be too hot to spend long, however.

REGULAR:
Air Seoul
Batik Air
Cebu Pacific
China Airlines
China Southern
Eastar Jet
Jeju Air
Jin Air
Lion Air
Lucky Air
Malindo Air
Philippines AirAsia
Royal Brunei
Shanghai Airlines
SilkAir
Spring Airlines
Wings Air
XiamenAir

KUALA LUMPUR INTERNATIONAL

KUL | WMKK

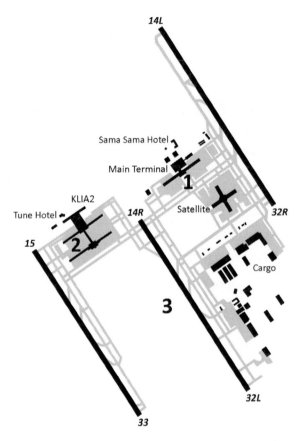

A large hub airport known to most as KLIA. It is one of Asia's busiest airports, and was opened in 1998, replacing the cramped Subang Airport close to the centre of the city.

It is the home base of Malaysia Airlines, AirAsia and AirAsia X and on the route network of many cargo airlines, as well as carriers from around the world.

The airport is split into two sections – KLIA1, which is the original complex, and KLIA2, which

BASE FOR:
AirAsia
AirAsia X
AsiaCargo Express
Malaysia Airlines
Malindo Air
MASkargo
UPS Airlines

↓

opened for low-cost operators in May 2014. Both main terminal buildings have official viewing facilities. KLIA1 has a satellite building, which doesn't have any spotting areas, although it is possible to view from certain gates. You can travel between the two areas using a train, which costs less than £1/$1.

KLIA has three runways and a large cargo complex. Arrivals and departures are predominantly in the 32/33 direction, with most of the low-cost airlines using runway 15/33 next to KLIA2. As well as the locations below, you can drive the perimeter roads to explore the best locations – but beware security may move you on.

Spotting Locations

1. KLIA 1 Terminal Viewing Gallery
Upstairs in the main terminal building, close to the food court, is an official viewing area. Situated indoors, this large room overlooks the airfield, including all gates at the main building, and some of those on the satellite terminal. The cargo area and KLIA2 are not really visible from this location, and the runways are a little distant, but most movements will be visible at some point. Photography can sometimes prove awkward because you're shooting through glass, but in general is quite good.

2. KLIA 2 Terminal Viewing Gallery
The viewing areas in KLIA2 can be found on level 3 departures. Follow the signs for the smoking area and food courts. You will come across the outside viewing area next to McDonald's. It is split into two sides, with each overlooking around nine different gates. The central parking area is not visible from the viewing area, but aircraft can be seen taxiing in and out from the left section. You can also see aircraft on the new runway 15/33 from here.

REGULAR:
Air Astana
Air China
Air Mauritius
All Nippon Airways
AsiaCargo Express
Bangkok Airways
Batik Air
Biman Bangladesh
British Airways
Cargolux
Cathay Dragon
Cebu Pacific
China Airlines
China Eastern
China Southern
Condor
Emirates
Ethiopian Airlines
Etihad
EVA Air
FedEx Express
Flynas
Garuda Indonesia
Himalaya Airlines
Hong Kong Airlines
Indonesia AirAsia
Iraqi Airways
Japan Airlines
Jetstar Asia Airways
KLM
Korean Air
Lion Air
Lucky Air
Mahan Air
Nepal Airlines
Oman Air
Pakistan International
Philippine Airlines
Philippines AirAsia
Qatar Airways
Regent Airways
Republic Express Airlines
Royal Brunei
Royal Jordanian
Saudia
Scoot
Shanghai Airlines

↓

3. Mound

A raised mound overlooking the airport and runway 14R/32L is a good spot for photography away from the terminals. You'll need a 300mm lens for aircraft of B737/A320 size. To reach the location, follow road 27 from the KLIA2 terminal around the perimeter and turn towards security post 6. Follow the road parallel to the airport fence, take the first left and then first right to reach the mound. You can drive up to reach the view.

Shenzhen Airlines
SilkAir
Silk Way Airlines
Singapore Airlines
SriLankan Airlines
Thai AirAsia
Thai Airways
Thai Smile
Turkish Airlines
Uni-Top Airlines
US-Bangla Airlines
Uzbekistan Airways
VietJet Air
Vietnam Airlines
XiamenAir

Spotting Hotels

Sama Sama Hotel

Jalan CTA 4 B, 64000 KLIA – Sepang, Selangor Darul Ehsan
+603 8787 3333 | www.samasamahotels.com

Located alongside KLIA 1, making it close enough to walk to the viewing area. Rooms on the top floors and facing the airport allow most movements to be seen, although they can be a little distant for photography or reading off.

Tune Hotel

Lot Pt 13, Jalan KLIA 2/2 6400 KLIA, Selangor Darul Ehsan
www.tunehotels.com

A new hotel built alongside the KLIA 2 low-cost terminal and connected via a covered walkway. Some rooms on the sixth floor face the nearest runway and associated taxiway. No gates can be seen at either KLIA1 or 2. Rooms get free WiFi.

OTHER AIRPORTS

Johor Bahru Senai International

JHB | WMKJ

Senai is a hub airport for AirAsia not far from Singapore, serving the city of Johor Bahru. It has a single runway and a small passenger terminal. Other airlines here include Firefly, Jin Air, Malaysia Airlines, Malindo Air and Thai AirAsia.

To the north of the terminal is a cargo facility used by MASkargo and Raya Airways, as well as an executive terminal. At the time of writing a couple of classic Boeing 747 aircraft were stored in this area.

Aside from the departure lounge, there are few viewing areas. If you have a car, drive north from the terminal towards the Palm Golf Resort. At the entrance, turn right (signposted Hutan Bandar Putra) and you'll soon parallel the northern end of the runway where photographs are possible if you park discretely.

Kuala Lumpur Sultan Abdul Aziz Shah (Subang)

SZB | WMSA

The original Kuala Lumpur Subang airport is still an operational airport, albeit a shadow of its former self. The main terminal was demolished when KLIA opened, but its former Terminal 3 is now operating as a terminal for passenger flights, with operators such as Firefly and Malindo Air providing domestic links. The airport is also home to a busy cargo terminal and maintenance base. Eurocopter Malaysia are also based here, as are some private jet operators.

The airport has a single runway, with facilities on either side.

The airport is around a 30-minute drive from KLIA, or can be reached from Sentral Station via bus. Some aircraft can be seen by driving or walking around the fence, but security may move you on. A café inside the terminal overlooks one of the parking ramps.

Kuching International

KCH | WBGG

A joint civil-military airport in the state of Sarawak. It has one runway, 07/25, with the terminal on the north side and military base on the south.

AirAsia in the main operator, along with Malaysia Airlines and Malindo Air. Regional cargo services are also common here with MASkargo, Transmile Air Services and other local carriers.

The Aeroville Mall just east of the airport (follow road 900B, then turn right towards Stutong) is a great place for watching runway 25 arrivals.

Langkawi International

LGK | WMKL

The airport serving the northern Malaysian resort island of Langkawi sees domestic flights, some links to China and occasional long-haul charters. Events at the neighbouring Mahsuri International Exhibition can also bring exotic visitors.

The airport has one runway which extends along the shoreline, giving some views from the beaches and road running parallel. There are opportunities to park up and take photographs through the fence.

Another spotting location is the Helang Hotel next to the passenger terminal. Many rooms have great views of the ramp.

Miri Airport

MYY | WBGR

Another modest airport on Sarawak. Miri has a small passenger terminal and a single runway, but handles over 2 million passengers per year mostly on domestic links to Kuala Lumpur and other parts of the country. AirAsia, Malaysia Airlines and Wings Air provide the movements. You can view from alongside the terminal, or once in the departure area.

Penang International

PEN | WMKP

Situated on the southern tip of Penang Island off Malaysia's western coast, Penang International is Malaysia's third busiest airport in terms of passengers with links around the country and Asia. All Malaysian carriers have a presence here, and interesting other airlines include Cathay Dragon, China Airlines Citilink, China Southern, Lion Air, Lucky Air, Qatar Airways, Scoot and Thai Smile.

Cargo is also a major part of Penang's operation, with a dedicated cargo terminal on the opposite side of the runway to the passenger terminal. Regular operators include Cathay Pacific, DHL, EVA Air, FedEx Express, Korean Air, MASkargo and UPS Airlines.

Most arrivals and departures use runway 04. If you have a car, and industrial and commercial area on the north east side of the airport has some good views of aircraft departures and those taxiing (through the fence). From the terminal follow signs for George Town and Tokong Ular on route 6. Then turn left on Jalan Mayang Pasir. Turn right on P8, then right onto route 6 again. After you cross the river, turn left immediately and follow the road round until you see the runway.

MONGOLIA

Capital: Ulan Bator

ULAN BATOR ●

Overview

Still one of the world's more remote countries. Its only international gateway is Chinggis Khan Airport at Ulan Bator, the country's capital. This airport is due to be replaced in 2019 by a new facility around 50km to the south, which has a modern new terminal and will not be as restricted.

International traffic to Mongolia is rising slowly, and it is hoped the new airport and growth of MIAT Mongolian Airlines will facilitate that. Perhaps it will become a more common spotting destination in the future.

ULAN BATOR CHINGGIS KHAAN INTERNATIONAL

ULN | ZMUB

The existing airport is located close to the city, but is restricted on space and has outdated facilities. It will be replaced by a new airport in 2019.

Visitors to the current site will find a small passenger terminal handling close to 1 million passengers per year, with a single runway and military facilities also on site. A number of retired aircraft can be seen scattered around the site, but only usually from on board an aircraft that is landing or departing.

Most movements are by the based airlines or those from neighbouring China and Russia.

Views are possible airside in the terminal. You can also see some aircraft from outside the terminal. Walk to the west and you'll find a preserved Ilyushin IL-14 nearby.

Naadamchdyn Zam road passes the northern end of the runway. An area of waste ground is good for watching aircraft arriving from the north (the only direction of arrival).

BASE FOR:
Aero Mongolia
Hunnu Air
MIAT Mongolian Airlines

REGULAR:
Aeroflot
Air Busan
Air China
IrAero
Korean Air
Turkish Airlines

OTHER AIRPORTS

Ulan Bator Chinggis Khaan International (new)

Due to open in early 2019, this new international facility is 52km south of the capital. It has one east-west runway and a modern passenger terminal on the north side. Initial views suggest no official spotting locations, but there are likely to be good views once airside in the terminal.

MYANMAR

Capital: Naypyidaw

MANDALAY

NAY PYI TAW

YANGON

Overview

Also known commonly as Burma, Myanmar is a popular tourist destination between China, India and Thailand. The capital at Yangon (Rangoon) has the busiest airport, served by the most international flights. Mandalay International is also a busy, modern airport. However, others in the country are quieter and served mostly by domestic flights.

The local airlines in Myanmar are not seen in too many places, so are worth getting into your logbook or camera lenses.

If you do venture away from the capital, plan a visit to the Defence Services Museum at Naypyidaw.

The Peoples Park in Yangon is also worth a visit, especially if visiting the neighbouring Scwedagon Pagoda. In the park you'll find five former Myanmar Airways Fokker F27 aircraft being used as playgrounds or simply languishing away.

PRINCIPAL AIRPORTS

YANGON INTERNATIONAL

RGN | VYYY

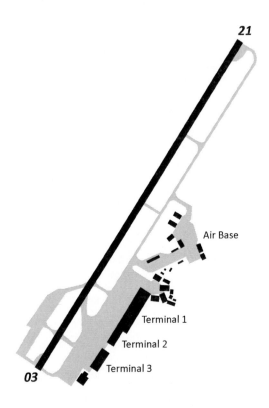

1

Myanmar's main international airport, serving the capital (also known as Rangoon), and located in the Mingaladon district around 15 miles north of the city. It has a single runway, 03/21, and three terminals.

Terminals 1 and 3 are both new structures, built in 2014 and 2016 respectively, to handle growth in demand at the airport. Terminal 2 is undergoing refurbishment at the time of writing. All three are located side-by-side at the southern end of the airport.

BASE FOR:
Air KBZ
Air Mandalay
Asian Wings Airways
Golden Myanmar Airlines
Myanmar International
Myanmar National

↓

Ultimately a new airport for Yangon, named Hanthawaddy International, will be opened in the early 2020s.

Much of the country's domestic airlines and their fleets pass through Yangon on a daily basis, so there is little need to venture to the outlying airports. However, Yangon is not the easiest place to spot at.

If travelling through the airport, you have good views once airside in the terminals, particularly of the runway and gates immediately in front. Aircraft at other terminals can evade you unless you remain vigilant.

The Palm Spring Resort (1) is also another good place to spot from (see next section).

Spotting Hotel

Palm Spring Resort

No. 7F, Nant Thar Gone Quarter, Insein Township, Yangon 11221 | +95 1 646 467 | www.palmspringresort.com.mm

A good standard hotel close to the airport. Aircraft depart or land directly overhead, and rooms in the range 510-514 have views toward the airport.

REGULAR:
Air China
Air India
AirAsia
All Nippon Airways
Bangkok Airways
Biman Bangladesh
Cathay Dragon
China Airlines
China Eastern
China Southern
Emirates
Jetstar Asia
Korean Air
Malaysia Airlines
Malindo Air
Mann Yatanarpon Airlines
Nok Air
Qatar Airways
SilkAir
Singapore Airlines
Thai AirAsia
Thai Airways
Thai Lion Air
Thai Smile
VietJet Air
Vietnam Airlines
Yangon Airways

OTHER AIRPORTS

Mandalay International

MDL | VYMD

Only opened in 1999, this is a modern international airport, but not as busy as Yangon. Its distance from the city is a bit of a problem. It has a heavy domestic fleet presence, as well as airlines like Air India, Bangkok Airways, China Eastern, Donghai Airlines, Sichuan Airlines, SilkAir, Thai AirAsia and Thai Smile.

Mandalay has a single north-south runway (the longest in Southeast Asia) and small terminal on the western side. There are good views from inside the terminal departure area, but no viewing areas outside.

Nay Pyi Taw International

NYT | VYNT

With a good central location in the country, between Yangon and Mandalay, Nay Pyi Taw is being built in stages to realise its potential as a future hub. It currently has one runway and a modern terminal, but expects a second runway and more buildings.

It is mostly served by the country's domestic airlines, with some flights into China and Thailand. There are views from the departure lounge.

MUSEUMS

Defence Services Museum

Zeyathiri Township, Naypyidaw | +95 9 796 255365

Half-way between Yangon and Mandalay, this huge museum occupies 600 acres with great views and interesting buildings. The aircraft collection includes a couple of Douglas DC-3s and a Fairchild Hiller FH-227 among other military types and vehicles. Open daily 9.30am-4.30pm.

NEPAL

Capital: Kathmandu

Overview

Nepal's location among the Himalayas makes it the main entry point for mountain climbers and adventurers tackling the famed region and world's tallest mountain, Everest.

The main entry point is Kathmandu airport, which sits surrounding by menacing mountains making its approach tricky. It handles flights from across Asia and parts of Europe and the Middle East. From there, visitors board the many domestic commuter flights to outlying airports. The most famous is Lukla, whose runway is perched on the edge of a cliff overlooking a deep valley. There is only one way in and one way out, and it can be very busy with smaller airliners like the DHC-6 Twin Otter and Dornier 228.

KATHMANDU TRIBHUVAN INTERNATIONAL

KTM | VNKT

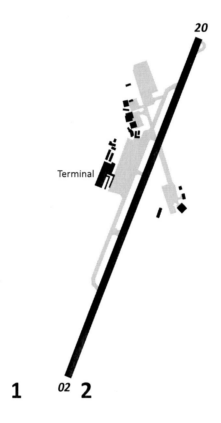

The main airport gateway to Nepal, serving the capital Kathmandu at an elevation of 4,390ft (1,338m). Its location makes the approach to the airport tricky, and has resulted in a number of accidents over the years.

Nevertheless, Kathmandu is served by many international carriers, and is also a transit point for onward travel to Everest and the Himalayas, including the airport of Lukla.

BASE FOR:
Buddha Air
Himalaya Airlines
Nepal Airlines
Shree Airlines
Saurya Airlines
Simirik Airlines
Sita Air
Tara Air
Yeti Airlines

Kathmandu has a single runway and both an international and domestic terminal, both located on the northern side of the runway. Many commuter aircraft park on the ramp outside the domestic terminal, and it is a good place to see the aircraft of smaller carriers shuttling passengers to and from the outlying regions of the country all in one place.

The airport is also home to the maintenance bases of carriers such as Nepal Airlines, Himalaya Airlines and Buddha Air.

Spotting around the southern end of the runway is the best option, with good opportunities for photography. However, you'd need to take a taxi to get there.

One spot is alongside the busy H03 road (1) which skirts the airport's southern boundary, close to the Shiva Temple.

The other spot (2) is in Jadibuti, on the eastern side. You can ask a taxi driver to take you there, and then look for the dirt road alongside the fence. It is possible to walk between both locations.

Security sometimes will ask you to stop taking pictures, but more often than not will turn a blind eye or not even notice you.

REGULAR:
Air Arabia
Air China
Air India
AirAsia X
Bhutan Airlines
Biman Bangladesh
Cathay Dragon
China Eastern
China Southern
Druk Air
Etihad
flydubai
IndiGo
Jet Airways
Korean Air
Malaysia Airlines
Malindo Air
Oman Air
Qatar Airways
Sichuan Airlines
SilkAir
Summit Air
Thai Airways
Thai Lion Air
Tibet Airlines
Turkish Airlines
Wataniya Airways

OTHER AIRPORTS

Lukla Tenzing-Hillary Airport

LUA | VNLK

With one way in and one way out, Lukla's airport is perched precariously on the edge of a cliff overlooking a deep valley. It is high up in the Himalayas and serves as a staging post for adventurers, climbers and walkers visiting the Mt Everest region. It sees a steady flurry or small commuter turboprops coming and going to Kathmandu all day – you might have seen videos of the action. The main viewpoint is behind runway 24 where a path leads to an elevated position overlooking the runway and parking apron.

MUSEUMS

Aviation Museum Nepal

Sinamangal, Kathmandu, Nepal | +977 9868 469 396 | www.nepalaviationmuseum.com

The new museum alongside Kathmandu Airport centres around a former Turkish Airlines Airbus A330 which ran off the runway at the airport in 2015, as well as a Fokker 100 aircraft. Visitors can go on board the aircraft, and see numerous other exhibits on aviation. Open daily.

NORTH KOREA

Capital: Pyongyang

Overview

One of the world's most secretive and reclusive countries, North Korea has
certainly had its fair share of media attention. Most recently a deal brokered
between itself and the United States could pave the way to the country
opening up more, and a relaxation of tensions.

Despite advice against travel to North Korea by many countries, enthusiasts
have long been visiting it for the opportunity to experience – and even fly on
– airliners rarely seen elsewhere before.

To visit the country, it is advisable only to do so through an organised tour
company who can arrange all aspects of travel for you, as well as flights on
the classic Soviet aircraft of national airline Air Koryo. One of the best-known
operators of such tours is Juche Travel Services (www.juchetravelservices.com).

With tensions thawing and the possibility of sanctions being lifted, we could
see Air Koryo updating its fleet with more modern types, which would make
visiting less appealing.

PYONGYANG INTERNATIONAL

FNJ | ZKPY

The main airport in North Korea, serving the capital. It is the base for Air Koryo and its fleet of old and young Russian airliners. Enthusiasts have had access in recent years through a number of organised tours, which has allowed ramp access to the small airport. However, spotting outside of these organised tours should not be attempted.

Pyongyang has a pair of runways, 01/19 and 17/35, however the latter has not been in use recently. There are two modern terminals which were opened in 2015 and 2016 respectively. The air base is on the western side of the airport.

BASE FOR:
Air Koryo

REGULAR:
Air China

OTHER AIRPORTS

Wonsan Kalma Airport

WOS | ZKWS

A joint civil-military airport on the east cost of North Korea. It includes a modern terminal which opened to passengers in 2015 when enthusiasts arrived on a charter from Pyongyang. Air Koryo operates domestic flights from here.

The Wonsan International Air Festival took place here in September 2016, which was a big draw for enthusiasts. However, the follow-up event was cancelled amid tensions. It may return in the future.

PHILIPPINES

Capital: Manila

Overview

Like Indonesia, the Philippines is a country which consists of thousands of islands and as a result its population relies on air travel heavily. There are many smaller airports scattered around these islands, served in the most part by just one or two routes to the country's larger airports at Manila and Cebu City.

The Philippines have been ready to embrace low cost travel. It is home to Cebu Pacific and Philippines AirAsia, along with the national carrier Philippine Airlines.

Many enthusiasts came to the country to visit the aircraft graveyard at Manila, however the collection here has somewhat dissipated in recent years.

PRINCIPAL AIRPORTS

MACTAN-CEBU INTERNATIONAL

CEB | RPVM

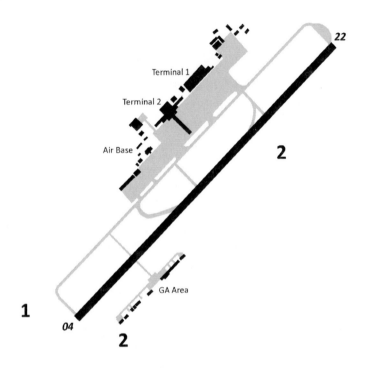

Situated on an island opposite the city of Cebu and linked by road bridges and ferries, this is the Philippines' second-busiest airport.

A former US air base, Cebu has a single, long runway. The two passenger terminals (the most recent opened in 2018) and the small Mactan Air Base are located on the northern side. A second, parallel runway will be built in the coming years.

Movements include a mix of low-cost airlines and domestic flights, along with links to other Asian and Middle Eastern countries. With some cargo flights and the military transport movements, it's an interesting airport to visit.

BASE FOR:
Cebgo
Cebu Pacific
PAL Express
Philippine Airlines
Philippines AirAsia

↓

Spotting Locations

1. Lapu Lapu City College

Take a taxi or hire a scooter to get to this college on Basak-Marigondon Rd. It looks out on the end of runway 04 and is perfect for approach and line-up shots on the afternoon. If the guard doesn't let you spot from within the college grounds, there is a vacant area alongside.

2. General Aviation Road

This road runs along the southern boundary of the airport, accessible just a little further on from spot 1. As the name suggests, it passes the general aviation area where many light aircraft are located. You can find various spots looking through the fence for runway shots and spotting. A wooden shelter near the 04 end is often used (tip the owner). Another good spot is the fire station, further up the road.

Spotting Hotel

Waterfront Airport Hotel & Casino

Airport Road Lapu Lapu Cebu , 6015, Cebu | +63 32 340 4888 | www.waterfronthotels.com.ph

Located just outside the terminals at Mactan-Cebu Airport. Rooms on the top floor are just high enough to look over the terminal buildings towards the taxiways and runway. A little awkward for photography, but you should see all movements.

REGULAR:
Air Busan
Air Juan
Asiana Airlines
Cathay Pacific
China Eastern
Emirates
EVA Air
FedEx Express
Jeju Air
Jin Air
Juneyao Airlines
Korean Air
Lucky Air
Okay Airways
Pan Pacific Airlines
Scoot
Sichuan Airlines
SilkAir
T'way Airlines
Tri-MG Intra Asia Airlines
Vanilla Air
XiamenAir

MANILA NINOY AQUINO INTERNATIONAL

MNL | RPLL

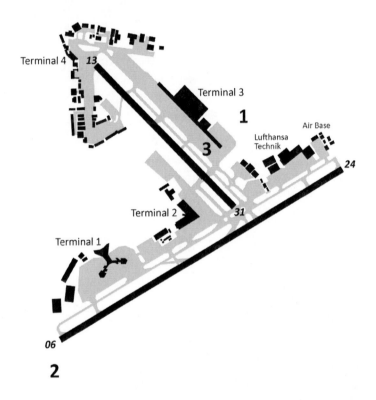

The principal airport in the Philippines and home to its indigenous airlines. Ninoy Aquino is a few miles south of the city centre and has two runways which cross close to their centre – 06/24 and 13/31. The majority of movements use the former.

The airport has four terminals – the newer Terminal 3 is on the north-east side of runway 13/31, while all others, including the older Terminal 4 domestic facility are on the south-west side.

BASE FOR:
Cebgo
Cebu Pacific
PAL Express
Philippine Airlines
Philippines AirAsia

↓

Further to the east is a Lufthansa Technik maintenance base which often has a number of heavy airliners present.

Around the northern side of the airport is a host of smaller hangars and companies engaging in flight training, maintenance, operations and cargo. It is this area which was always of interest to enthusiasts as many smaller types operate from here, and for years a collection of rusting old airliners was stored. Some are still present, but not on the scale of the past.

Manila is not as busy as other Asian hubs like Hong Kong or Tokyo's airports, but can still get crowded and offers a good variety of airliners and in particular the domestic traffic not seen elsewhere. There are good views from the departure areas of the terminals.

Spotting Locations

1. Holiday Inn Express
Perhaps the easiest and least conspicuous area (see later).

2. Runway 06 Arrivals
If you have a car or walk 25 minutes, this is a great spot for arrivals on runway 06, which is the primary direction of traffic. You can't see the rest of the airport, apart from aircraft lining up for departure. Photography is great here. To reach this location from Terminal 1, walk along the Paranaque – Sucat Road, then turn south along Multinational Ave (where you see the brown metal footbridge crossing the road. Walk past the end of the runway and find a good spot – often there are local spotters here.

3. Terminal 3
Inside this terminal there is a new walkway signposted 'Airport Runway' on the 4th floor, near the food court. There are no seats, but you can use the windows for a quick view of anything outside.

REGULAR:
Air China
Air Juan
Air Hong Kong
Air Niugini
AirAsia
All Nippon Airways
Asiana Airlines
Cathay Pacific
China Airlines
China Eastern
China Southern
Delta
Emirates
Ethiopian Airlines
Etihad
EVA Air
FedEx Express
Gulf Air
Hong Kong Airlines
Japan Airlines
Jeju Air
Jetstar Asia
Jetstar Japan
KLM
Korean Air
Kuwait Airways
Lucky Air
Malaysia Airlines
Oman Air
Qantas
Qatar Airways
Royal Brunei
Saudia
Shenzhen Airlines
Singapore Airlines
SkyJet
Thai Airways
Turkish Airlines
ULS Airlines Cargo
United Airlines
XiamenAir

Spotting Hotel

Holiday Inn Express Manila Airport

Newport Boulevard, Pasay 1309 Metro Manila | +63 2 908 8600 | www.ihg.com

Formerly the Remington Hotel. This hotel is excellent if you get a good room overlooking the airport. Generally, rooms on the fifth floor upwards in the range xx009-xx0017 and xx0068-xx0073 will be perfect. Photography is possible from the rooms of aircraft on the nearby taxiway and runway. It is also next to the Air Force Museum.

OTHER AIRPORTS

Clark International

CRK | RPLC

The former Clark Air Force Base used by the US Air Force as a major Asian outpost is now a civil airport at Angeles City to the north of Manila. Construction work is underway to develop its terminal facilities as a viable alternative to the capital's airport, with ambitions to see over 100 million passengers per year.

At present, Clark has airline flights from the likes of Asiana, Cathay Dragon, Cebu Pacific, Emirates, Jetstar, Philippine Airlines, Qatar Airways and Scoot. It is also a busy cargo hub, with UPS Airlines operating a base here.

A storage area on the northern side of the site is home to various decaying airliners and commuter aircraft. You can see them from the taxi rank outside the current terminal.

Exploring the smaller roads south of the terminal you'll have fleeting views to the cargo and military ramp, and also find the Air Force Park with a number of preserved military types on display.

Davao Francisco Bangoy International

DVO | RPMD

Serving Davao City at the southern end of the Philippines archipelago, this airport has a single runway and modest passenger terminal, with a smaller cargo terminal alongside. Airlines include AirAsia, Cathay Dragon, Cebu Pacific, Philippine Airlines and SilkAir.

Spotting locations exist in the residential areas around either end of the runway, but require some local knowledge and access to a car to reach them. Elsewhere, some views are possible either side of the terminal.

Kalibo International

KLO | RPVK

An airport serving some 2.7 million passengers per year – mostly on domestic links, but with international carriers Air Busan, Air Seoul, China Airlines, Jin Air, Juneyao Airlines, Okay Airways, Scoot, Sichuan Airlines and XiamenAir all regular visitors – particularly on seasonal routes.

The airport is quite compact, with one runway and a small parking apron outside the terminal at the northern end.

A short walk from the terminal leads to the main road passing the northern end of the runway. You can see any airliners parked on the apron here, as well as runway movements.

MUSEUMS

Philippine Air Force Aerospace Museum

Nr Andrews Ave, Pasay City, Manila | +63 2832 3498 | www.paf.mil.ph

Located near Terminal 3, on the Villamor Air Base side of the airport. This museum has around 20 aircraft on display, including both fighters and transport types. Open 8am-5pm Monday to Friday, 8am-12pm Saturday.

RUSSIA (EASTERN)

Capital: Moscow

Overview

This section concerns the easternmost part of Russia which occupies Asia – known widely as Siberia, along with the parts closest to China, Japan, the Koreas and Alaska.

Russia has always held a draw for enthusiasts owing to the vast numbers of Soviet-built aircraft which would work in the country. Many still exist, however airlines have largely upgraded to modern Western aircraft.

Spotting in Russia comes with its risks, but is not impossible and some airports even encourage organised visits. You may wish to arrange one of these in advance, or join an overseas spotting tour, or simply try your luck visiting one of eastern Russia's airports within easy reach of the rest of Asia.

Here are some of the highlights.

PRINCIPAL AIRPORTS

VLADIVOSTOK INTERNATIONAL

VVO | UHWW

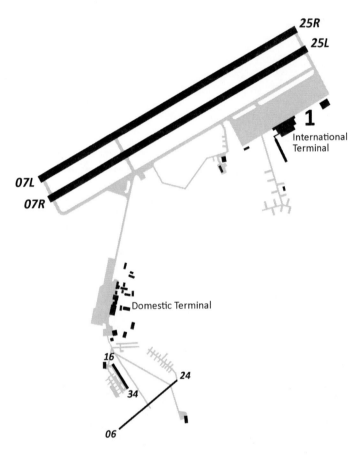

25R
25L
1
International Terminal
07L
07R
Domestic Terminal
16
24
34
06

Vladivostok is the closest major Russian airport to the hubs of the Far East. It is only a short distance across the sea from Japan, and close to the land borders with China and North Korea. It handles flights from all across the Far East, as well as links to Moscow and other Russian hubs, plus local communities within the region.

BASE FOR:
Auroria
S7 Airlines

↓

The airport has a pair of main parallel runways and a modern terminal area to the east. In the south of the site is the older domestic terminal, plus a military and general aviation area with two smaller runways. An express train links the newer international terminal with the city.

Just outside the international terminal you'll see a preserved Yakovlev Yak-40. From here you can see some aircraft parked at the gates (1). There are also views from the departure lounge.

There are a number of retired airliners and transport aircraft around the airport, particularly around the military area, but these are difficult (likely impossible) to see from the ground.

Vladivostok has been hosting an annual 'Spotters Day' in recent years, organised by the airport's Press Center (see www.vvo.aero). This gives spotters the chance to go airside and photograph aircraft from various vantage points. Visiting at other times can be arranged through the website, with spotters accompanied by an airport representative.

REGULAR:
Aeroflot
Air Busan
Air Koryo
China Express Airlines
China Southern
Eastar Jet
IrAero
Jeju Air
Korean Air
Nordwind Airlines
Rossiya Airlines
Sichuan Airlines
T'way Air
Tianjin Airlines
Ural Airlines
Yakutia Airlines

OTHER AIRPORTS

Magadan Sokol Airport

GDX | UHMM

A regional airport serving the port city on the Sea of Okhotsk, north of Japan. Sokol Airport has one runway, with a small passenger terminal on the north side. It is served by Aeroflot, Aurora, IrAero, Rossiya Airlines and Yakutia Airlines. There is a preserved Antonov An-12 outside the terminal, and some stored airliners to the east and west, which are visible in the distance from the departure lounge, or fleetingly through the trees from the access roads.

Petropavlovsk-Kamchatsky Airport

PKC | UHPP

A vital outpost in the distant east of Russia, Petropavlovsk-Kamchatsky is a moderately busy regional airport served by Aeroflot, Aurora, Rossiya Airlines, S7 Airlines, Ural Airlines and Yakutia. The latter operates a seasonal service to Anchorage, AK.

Local operator Petropavlovsk-Kamchatsky Air Enterprise is based here and flies older Soviet types on regional routes.

The airport is also an active military base for fighter and transport squadrons, with many aircraft in storage at the site – albeit largely hidden from view among the tress in far corners of the airfield. A window view from a departing aircraft might help spot some of them.

A small park next to the passenger terminal has good views across the parking apron.

Yakutsk Airport

YKS | UEEE

Yakutsk is a land-locked city in central Siberia which can be incredibly cold in winter. It is home to Yakutia Airlines, and the airport is a vital link to the many outlying communities in Siberia. It has links to other major airports in Russia and some in China and South Korea.

If you venture to Yakutsk, you'll see various stored and retired aircraft around the site, and various cargo aircraft used to supply the region. Just near the terminal is a preserved Yak-40 and Antonov An-24.

A few miles west of Yakutia is Magan Airport, which is a busy general aviation field and also used as a testing site by Boeing on occasion.

SINGAPORE

Capital: Singapore

SELETAR

PAYA LEBAR

SINGAPORE CHANGI

Overview

Off the southern tip of Malaysia, and just across the sea from Indonesia, Singapore is a fantastic city state worth visiting for many reasons. For enthusiasts, its huge Changi Airport is one of the most important hubs in the world and should be tried, not least because it caters for enthusiasts and has some great hotels to spot from.

Elsewhere on the small islands you'll find two other airports of note – Paya Lebar Air Base, which used to be the main commercial airport, and Seletar Airport which often has a few interesting aircraft present.

Singapore is a safe country to visit, and any form of lawlessness is treated very harshly. English is spoken as standard and the transport infrastructure is efficient.

SINGAPORE CHANGI

SIN | WSSS

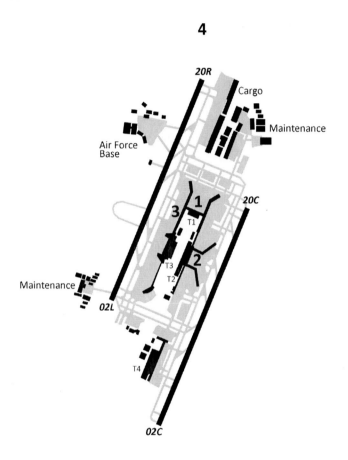

Singapore's Changi Airport is one of the world's largest aviation hubs, and a major transit point for travellers heading between Europe and Asia. It is home to Singapore Airlines and its cargo division, plus its Scoot and Silk Way low-cost offshoots. The airport is never quiet and offers a really interesting mix for the enthusiast, with many smaller regional Asian carriers coming and going regularly among the big international traffic.

BASE FOR:
FedEx Express
Jetstar Asia
Scoot
SilkAir
Singapore Airlines

↓

The airport layout is based around two parallel runways, with all of the terminals located in the central area between. After undergoing plenty of transformation recently, there are now four terminals in use, with another under construction alongside the new Jewel multi-use interconnecting structure which will add retail, entertainment and dining options for both passengers and visitors. The amenities and quality of the facilities here have ensured Changi is consistently voted the best in the world by passengers.

On the western side of the airport is a small site used by the Singapore Air Force, largely hidden by trees. You can often see its Fokker 50 and KC-130 aircraft arriving and departing, however.

In addition to being one of the busiest airports in the world for passengers, Changi is also a busy cargo hub, using a large complex of facilities to the north of the terminals, as well as Singapore Airlines' engineering hangars.

Thankfully there are a number of good spotting opportunities at the airport and enthusiasts can often be seen using them.

Spotting Locations

1. Terminal 1 Viewing Mall
Nicely air-conditioned, you can enjoy some good views of movements from this indoor area inside Terminal 1. It has views of the central apron and more distant views of aircraft on the runways. Singapore Airlines aircraft don't usually park here. Photography is acceptable, but through glass, and better on the afternoon. To reach the area, go up the escalators from the check-in hall.

2. Terminal 2 Viewing Mall
Smaller than the Terminal 1 Mall, this is another indoor room which looks out over parking stands used by Singapore Airlines and some other airlines, plus runway 02C/20C. You can reach

REGULAR:
AirBridgeCargo
Air China
Air France
Air Hong Kong
Air India
Air India Express
Air Mauritius
Air New Zealand
Air Niugini
AirAsia
All Nippon Airways
Asiana Airlines
ASL Airlines Belgium
Bangkok Airways
Batik Air
Biman Bangladesh
British Airways
Cardig Air
Cargolux
Cathay Pacific
Cebu Pacific
China Airlines
China Cargo Airlines
China Eastern
China Southern
Delta
DHL Aviation
Druk Air
Emirates
Ethiopian Airlines
Etihad
EVA Air
Fiji Airways
Finnair
Garuda Indonesia
Hebei Airlines
Hong Kong Airlines
IndiGo
Indonesia AirAsia
Japan Airlines
JC International
Jet Airways
Jetstar Airways
Jetstar Pacific
KLM
Korean Air
K-Mile Air
Lion Air
LOT Polish Airlines
Lufthansa

↓

this area by heading up the escalators to the floor above departures, following the signs. Again, photography is possible through glass.

3. Terminal 3 Viewing Mall
This indoor area looks out over runway 02L/20R, which is usually the arrivals runway. Photography is not good here, but you can still log movements with ease. Reach the area from the check-in area via escalators, following the signs.

4. Changi Beach Park
If aircraft are arriving on runway 20R, head to the beach area north of the airport for great approach shots. You can move further down depending on the position of the sun. You can park at the ferry terminal, and there are bus stops here (take the 34 or 53 bus from the airport to Tampines Ave, then 9 bus to the ferry terminal).

Spotting Hotels

Crowne Plaza
75 Airport Boulevard #01-01, Singapore 819664
+65 6823 5354 | www.crowneplaza.com

The best hotel for spotting at Singapore Changi, but can be expensive. Views from the even numbered rooms are excellent if you get one on floors 7, 8 or 9 facing the airport (ask for a runway view). You will have views of some Terminal 3 gates and runway 02L/20R. Corridors can also be used for views of the central terminal area.

Changi Village Hotel
1 Netheravon Road, Singapore 508502
+65 6379 7111 | www.villagehotelchangi.com.sg

If you ask for a room facing the sea, you will be able to read off arriving aircraft landing on runway 20R and see aircraft using 20L, or 02L/R. You'll need flight tracking websites for night-time movements.

Malaysia Airlines
Malindo Air
Myanmar Airways
My Indo Airlines
Neptune Air
Nippon Cargo
Norwegian
Philippine Airlines
Philippines AirAsia
Qantas
Qatar Airways
Regent Airways
Royal Brunei
Saudia
Shenzhen Airlines
Sichuan Airlines
Silk Way West Airlines
Spring Airlines
SriLankan Airlines
Swiss International
Thai AirAsia
Thai Airways
Thai Lion Air
Transmile Air Services
Tri-MG Intra Asia Airlines
Turkish Airlines
United Airlines
UPS Airlines
US-Bangla Airlines
Uzbekistan Airways
VietJet Air
Vietnam Airlines
West Air
XiamenAir

OTHER AIRPORTS

Paya Lebar Air Base

QPG | WSAP

Paya Lebar operated as Singapore International Airport between 1954-1980, when Changi opened. Today it is a base of the Republic of Singapore Air Force, and home to the Air Force Museum (see later). Various squadrons of fighter jets and C-130 Hercules operate from here. Enthusiasts of a civil nature will be interested in regular VIP movements, plus large aircraft coming in for maintenance and cargo conversions. It is anticipated that Paya Lebar will close around 2030.

Due to the military nature of the airport, you are best spotting from the museum, which has views of some parts of the airfield and maintenance hangars.

Seletar Airport

XSP | WSSL

Originally a Royal Air Force base, built in 1928. Seletar later developed as a civil airport. Today it is mainly a general aviation facility, but many executive jets use it also and are scattered around the aprons on either side of the runway. There are maintenance companies based here usually working on turboprop types, biz jets, and occasionally larger airliners.

Development of Seletar into a passenger airport has been a long-running debate in Singapore, and a new terminal opened in 2018 with scheduled turboprop flights by Firefly moving here from Changi, relieving some of the pressure on the main airport.

Seletar is around 10 miles north-west of Changi. With a car, some views are possible from the road leading to the terminal. You can also walk along both sides and see many of the parked aircraft through the fence, but don't loiter for too long.

MUSEUMS

Air Force Museum

400 Airport Road, Singapore 534234 | +64 6461 8504

A nice exhibition of the history of the Royal Singapore Air Force located at Paya Lebar Air Base, around 9 miles from Changi. It features both indoor and outdoor exhibits with an interesting wing-shaped display building. There are no civil aircraft on display. Museum is open Tue-Sun, 8.30am-5pm. Free admission.

SOUTH KOREA

Capital: Seoul

Overview

South Korea is a relatively small county, but its population have long relied on air travel as a means of getting around. It therefore has a thriving domestic network and many indigenous airlines plying routes between the country's areas of population and smaller airports. The route between Seoul and Jeju Island is the busiest air route in the world.

Much of the country's aviation is centred around the two airports at Seoul – Gimpo and Incheon, which handle mostly domestic and international services respectively. There are a lot of smaller airports that could be mentioned in this guide, but any enthusiast – particularly on a first visit – can usually log much of the country's domestic fleets and see any interesting overseas carriers on a visit to these two airports without the need to travel elsewhere.

Spotting in South Korea is quite common, but still fairly misunderstood and you might be asked what you are doing if you venture away from official viewing areas.

SEOUL GIMPO

GMP | RKSS

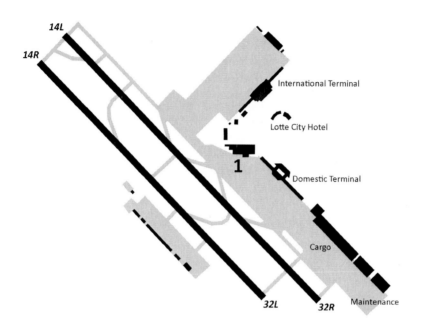

Gimpo is Seoul's original airport, and today is the busy domestic gateway for the capital. Movements are dominated by Asiana Airlines and Korean Air, along with other domestic carriers such as Air Busan, Eastar Jet, Jeju Air and T'way Airlines. Over a hundred flights a day link Gimpo with Jeju Island – the world's busiest air route. Many aircraft operate here which will not be seen at Incheon or outside the country, so it is worth the visit. Some international flights are allowed, particularly to China, Japan and Taiwan through Air China, All Nippon Airways, China Airlines, China Eastern, China Southern and Shanghai Airlines. Domestic aircraft tend to repeat after a few hours.

BASE FOR:
Asiana Airlines
Korean Air

↓

The airport has two parallel runways and two terminals at right angles to each other. A Korean Air maintenance and cargo base are to the south-east. General aviation and helicopters use facilities on the south-western side of the runways.

Spotting Location

1. Observation Deck
An observation deck with both indoor and outdoor areas can be found on the sixth floor of the Korea Airport Corporation building between the domestic and international terminals (the entrance is alongside a supermarket). It is good for logging all movements on the parallel runways and aprons, and is also fairly good for photography. It is open from 9am to 5pm, and closed Mondays.

Spotting Hotel

Lotte City Hotel Gimpo Airport
38, Haneul-gil, Gangseo-gu, Seoul | +82 2 6116 1000
www.lottehotel.com

Some of the rooms at this modern hotel have great views over the terminal buildings to the parking aprons and runways beyond. A little too distant for photography, and you may need flight trackers for some aircraft. But the best option here by far.

REGULAR:
Air Busan
Air China
All Nippon Airways
China Airlines
China Eastern
China Southern
Eastar Jet
EVA Air
Japan Airlines
Jeju Air
Jin Air
Shanghai Airlines
T'way Airlines

SEOUL INCHEON

ICN | RKSI

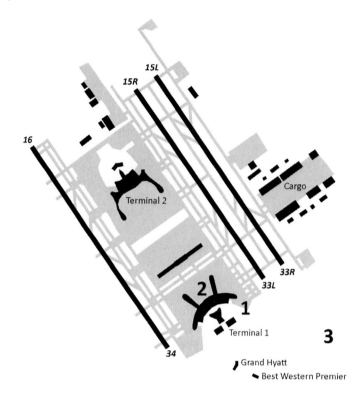

Seoul Incheon was opened in March 2001 after it became apparent that Gimpo airport was bursting at the seams and unable to expand. Incheon is a modern airport and has recently opened its new Terminal 2 and a third parallel runway. Passenger traffic is busy, with a heavy presence of both Korean Air and Asiana Airlines. Elsewhere, the airport has six cargo terminals on the northern side of the airport, which proves to be a very busy operation.

Security in South Korea is very tight and aircraft spotters are not officially tolerated. Therefore, beware that you are likely to be moved on or told to stop spotting by security personnel. Using

BASE FOR:
Air Incheon
Air Seoul
Asiana Airlines
Eastar Jet
FedEx Express
Jeju Air
Jin Air
Korean Air
Polar Air Cargo

↓

binoculars, poles and cameras can add suspicion, so be very discrete. Nevertheless, if you are departing from Incheon you can easily walk past most gates logging aircraft parked there.

The airport's website helpfully gives arrival information for all aircraft, including cargo flights.

Spotting Locations

1. Outside Domestic Terminal
Just outside the domestic part of Terminal 1 there is a smoking area which offers some views over the domestic gates and aircraft approaching runways 33L/R. You can also see aircraft departing in the opposite direction. It is possible to take photographs discretely from here.

2. Panorama Restaurant
Up on the 4th floor of the international part of Terminal 1 is the Panorama Restaurant which has views out over the gates around the terminal, and across to the satellite concourse. You must buy food and drink if you wish to stay here, and it can be quite expensive.

3. Park
A park directly under the approach to the northern runways is a short drive/taxi ride or a 30 minute walk from Terminal 1. It has benches and is popular with locals. You can easily take photographs of aircraft when landing from the south, but much of the airport is out of sight.

Spotting Hotels

Grand Hyatt Incheon Hotel
208 Yeongjonghaeannam-ro, 321 Beon-gil, Unseo-dong, Jung-gu, Incheon 400-719 | +82 32 745 1234
incheon.grand.hyatt.com

Located close to the end of runway 33, rooms facing the airport have views of this. Aircraft are quite far, so need a good pair of binoculars to read

REGULAR:
Aeroflot
Aeromexico
AirAsia X
Air Astana
Air Canada
Air China
Air France
Air India
Air Macau
AirBridgeCargo
Alitalia
American Airlines
ANA Cargo
British Airways
Cargolux
Cathay Pacific
Cebu Pacific
Centurion Air Cargo
China Airlines
China Cargo Airlines
China Eastern
China Postal Airlines
China Southern
Czech Airlines
Delta Air Lines
DHL Aviation
Emirates
Ethiopian Airlines
Etihad
EVA Air
Finnair
Garuda Indonesia
Hawaiian Airlines
Hong Kong Airlines
HK Express
JC International
Jetstar Pacific
KLM
Lao Airlines
Lion Air
LOT Polish Airlines
Lufthansa
Malaysia Airlines
Mandarin Airlines
MIAT Mongolian
Myanmar Airways
International
Nippon Cargo
Okay Airways Cargo

↓

off. The hotel is fairly expensive. There is a free shuttle bus to the terminal.

Best Western Premier Hotel Incheon Airport
48-27 Gonghang-ro 424beon-gil, Jung-gu, Incheon
+82 32 743 1000 | www.airportshotel.co.kr/en

Located in a similar position to the Hyatt, it is a little more reasonable but offers views of runway 33L and some views of the terminals from some rooms on floors 9 and 10. In-room TVs have a channel listing arrivals and departures, including cargo and GA movements.

Pan Pacific Airlines
Peach Aviation
Philippine Airlines
Philippines AirAsia
Qantas Freight
Qatar Airways
Royal Brunei
S7 Airlines
Scoot
SF Airlines
Shandong Airlines
Shenzhen Airlines
Sichuan Airlines
Silk Way Airlines
Singapore Airlines
Sky Angkor Airlines
Spring Airlines
Suparna Airlines
Thai AirAsia X
Thai Airways
Tianjin Airlines
Turkish Airlines
T'way Air
Uni Air
United Airlines
UPS Airlines
Uzbekistan Airways
VietJet Air
Vietnam Airlines
Volga-Dnepr Airlines
XiamenAir
Yakutia Airlines

OTHER AIRPORTS

Busan Gimhae International

PUS | RKPK

Situated to the west of Busan, and home to Air Busan. This airport is busy for domestic flights, and sees international service from most of China's carriers, plus Aeroflot, Cathay Dragon, HK Express, Japan Airlines, Lao Airlines, Lion Air, MIAT Mongolian, Peach, Philippine Airlines, Tigerair Taiwan, Thai and Vietnam Airlines among others.

The airport has two parallel runways and a modern international terminal. More expansion work is due to take place to help cope with growing passenger numbers. Gimhae Air Base is also located here, taking up much of the northern and eastern side of the airfield. On the western side there is a maintenance base used by Korean Air, often with some aircraft parked outside.

If you have a car, the southern end of the airport is good for watching and photographing arriving aircraft. There are also good views from within the terminals once airside.

There are some preserved aircraft visible when you drive past the military base.

Cheongju International

CJJ | RKTU

Cheongju is a busy domestic airport in the centre of the country. It has two parallel runways, a single passenger terminal, and a cargo apron. Much of the airport site is occupied by the Republic of Korea Air Force, with a based fighter jet wing.

Domestic airlines Asiana, Jeju Air, Jin Air and Korean Air dominate, with some international services by China Southern, Eastar Jet and Yakutia Airlines. There are some views from the car park alongside the terminal, and also once airside.

Daegu International

TAE | RKTN

Handling mostly domestic flights and some services from China, Taiwan and Vietnam, Daegu is the largest and busiest airport in the southern part of the country. It has two runways, with the terminal at the north-western end. The rest of the site is occupied by the air force.

A shopping mall near the northern end of the parallel runways is good for discrete arrival viewing. It is a short distance from the terminal.

There is a preserved Douglas C-54 among the air base complex, visible from departing aircraft.

Jeju International

CJU | RKPC

The air route between Seoul and the island of Jeju is the busiest in the world, with a great number of flights every day operated by many domestic airlines. Close to 30 million passengers used the airport last year, making it the second busiest in South Korea. However, much of what you can see here you will also see at Seoul's two airports.

The resident Jeju Air is naturally a dominant carrier, alongside Air Busan, Asiana, Jin Air and Korean Air. However, traffic is also made up of international carriers such as AirAsia X, Air China, Cathay Dragon, China Eastern, China Southern, HK Express, Philippine Airlines, Shenzhen Airlines, Spring Airlines and Tianjin Airlines.

It's possible to watch the aircraft coming and going from the seashore near Jeju City, as well as from a few spots on the road running alongside the main runway. There are also excellent views inside the terminal for departing passengers.

MUSEUMS

Jeju Aerospace Museum

218, Nokchabunjae-ro, Andeok-myeon, Seogwipo-si, Jeju-do | www.jdc-jam.com

Exhibits from the history of the Korean air force, plus space exploration. Includes a number of transport aircraft types. Open daily 9am-6pm.

SRI LANKA

Capital: Colombo

Overview

The island off the southern tip of India is home to a number of small airports which are all linked to the capital and main gateway at Colombo. Colombo actually has two airports – the domestic Ratmalana airport and international Bandaranaike airport.

It's worth visiting both of these airports, but the rest of the country may prove difficult to go spotting at, and the hobby is not generally understood, so it's best to keep safe.

PRINCIPAL AIRPORTS

COLOMBO RATMALANA

CMB | VCBI

Taking over as Colombo's main airport in the 1960s, this is now a fairly busy facility with one runway and two terminals. A second runway is planned, and a new international terminal will open in 2019. All facilities, including a cargo terminal, are on the south side of the runway. However, a small military facility can be found on the northern side, out of sight from the terminals.

The airport handles close to 10 million passengers per year – mostly through SriLankan Airlines and regional flights around the Indian sub-continent.

There are no official places to spot at Colombo, and security is tight with the site being used for military as well as civilian flights.

There are views, however, from within the departure areas of the terminals where you can easily log movements if you do it discretely.

BASE FOR:
Cinnamon Air
Millennium Airlines
SirLankan Airlines

REGULAR:
Aeroflot
Air Arabia
Air China
Air India
AirAsia
Cathay Pacific
China Eastern
China Southern
Emirates
Etihad
flydubai
Gulf Air
IndiGo
Jet Airways
KLM
Korean Air
Kuwait Airways
Malaysia Airlines
Malindo Air
Oman Air
Qatar Airways
Rotana Jet
Saudia
SilkAir
Singapore Airlines
SpiceJet
Sriwijaya Air
Thai Airways
Turkish Airlines
Ukraine International

OTHER AIRPORTS

Colombo Ratmalana

RML | VCCC

The oldest airport in Sri Lanka, and formerly the main gateway to Colombo. Today Ratmalana is a domestic and reliever airport to the main international facility to the north of the city.

Ratmalana is close to the centre of Colombo. It has a single runway, 04/22, with the main terminal and parking apron on the south side. You'll also find the Sri Lanka Air Force Museum here (see later).

Lots of domestic and air taxi operators fly from this airport, linking it to other parts of the country. Most are operated by small turboprops and helicopters. There are also cargo flights.

There are views from the access road as it runs alongside the runway. You also have some views from the museum.

Mattala Rajapaksa International

HRI | VCRI

A regional airport in the south of the island, serving Hambantota. It only opened in 2013, and initially enjoyed flights by SriLankan and flydubai, but at the time of writing has no scheduled passenger services. FitsAir operates cargo flights, and you will often see local aircraft, executive jets, and occasionally other freighters (the Antonov An-225 has visited). There are some distant views from the roads approaching the terminal.

MUSEUMS

Sri Lanka Air Force Museum

New Airport Rd, Dehiwala-Mount Lavinia, Sri Lanka | +94 77 244 4445
www.airforcemuseum.lk

Sri Lanka's only aviation museum of note, dedicated to the history of its air force. It is located alongside Ratmalana Airport in Colombo. The museum covers a large site with a good selection of interesting airframes parked both inside and out, including transport types. Open daily except Monday, 8.30am-4.30pm.

TAIWAN

Capital: Taipei

Overview

Taiwan, or the Republic of China as it is officially known, is the populous and relatively Western islands off the cost of mainland China.

Traditionally its population relied on an intense network of domestic services and airlines to get around, but over the past decade this has steadily declined with the advancement of a fast rail network and improved roads. Therefore, the variety of domestic aircraft once seen is now somewhat diminished.

However, there is still plenty to see, particularly at the two airports in the capital, Taipei, and Kaohsiung in the south.

PRINCIPAL AIRPORTS

TAIPEI SONGSHAN

TSA | RCSS

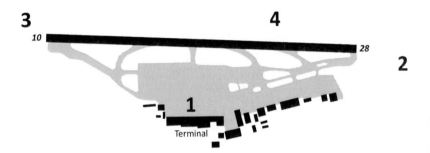

Taipei's original airport, close to downtown, transitioned into a mostly domestic facility from 1979 when Taoyuan Airport opened. This grew into a significant operation before the decline of domestic air travel in Taiwan.

Today the airport is still a hub for domestic flights, with both Far Eastern Air Transport and Uni Air based here. However, it also now sees a good number of international flights across the Taiwan Strait to China, and north to Japan.

The airport shares its single east-west runway with Songshan Air Base. The facilities are located immediately east of the passenger terminals, and mostly sees transport operations such as those to move the President and his government. Look out for a preserved Douglas DC-3 just outside the base.

BASE FOR:
Far Eastern Air Transport
Uni Air

REGULAR:
Air China
All Nippon Airways
China Airlines
China Eastern
Eastar Jet
EVA Air
Japan Airlines
Mandarin Airlines
Shanghai Airlines
Sichuan Airlines
T'way Air
XiamenAir

Spotting Locations

1. Observation Deck
Accessed upstairs between the domestic and international terminals and signposted clearly. This viewing area has great views over the terminal gates and runway. Photography is through tinted glass unfortunately. There are toilet and refreshment facilities next to the deck. Free to enter

2. Guanshan Riverside Park
When arrivals are on runway 28, this park next to the Keelung River is perfect for approach shots, and you can see aircraft lining up on the ground for departure. The park is popular with locals and safe during the day. It has a car park, or you could hire a bike from the MRT station at the airport to get there.

3. Runway 10
A popular spot with locals at the other end of the runway is the road which runs along the perimeter fence. You can get elevated views over the western side of the field, and see aircraft approaching and departing runway 10. The terminal area is not in view.

The nearby Agricultural Market has a car park, and is served by buses 49, 74, 642 and 643 from the airport. From there this spot is a 5-minute walk.

4. Air Force One Coffee
A café and restaurant on the north side of the airport, close to the runway. It has an elevated, outdoor viewing area which is good for photography (albeit backlit a lot of the time) and spotting aircraft parked at the terminal and air base. Spotters are welcome, just remember to buy food and drinks.

Public Transport: Songshan is connected to the MRT metro system. You can connect between Taipei Songshan and Taoyuan airports direct using bus #1840. It takes 40-60 minutes depending on traffic.

TAIPEI TAOYUAN

TPE | RCTP

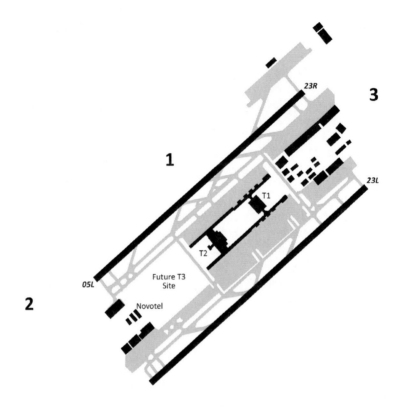

Taouuan is Taiwan's modern mega-hub, which is located 25 miles west of the city and the original Songshan airport. It is served by airlines from all over the world, with a heavy focus on traffic from the Far East. Almost 45 million passengers used the airport in 2017, with 246,000 aircraft movements.

The airport has a pair of parallel runways, the northerly of which was opened in 2015. In between you'll find the airport's two passenger terminals, with gates facing both runways. A third terminal is expected to open in 2020 which will greatly expand the airport's passenger capacity.

BASE FOR:
China Airlines
EVA Air
Uni Air
Tigerair Taiwan

↓

Taoyuan is also one of the world's busiest cargo hubs, with areas to the north and south of the terminals used by freighters. There are also maintenance bases and hangars for based and visiting airlines.

Spotting Locations

1. Miracle Café
On the north side of the airfield you'll find the "Miracle" Café, named due to it narrowly escaping damage when an Airbus A300 crashed alongside. It has views over the northern side of the airfield, and from its rooftop you can take acceptable photographs from afternoon till sunset. The cafe is situated on highway 15 road running along the northern perimeter, with parking outside the EMC car garage which uses the same building.

2. Runway 05L Sports Park
You'll need to drive to this location, which is close to highway 15 and next to the approach path to runway 05L. You have good photographic opportunities. There is a car park at the sports field which you can use.

3. Runway 23 approach
At the north eastern end of the airport there are locations which are good for runway 23L and R arrivals depending on the time of day. It's best to drive there, where you'll find the bridge over the river (Hangxiang Road), next to the DoDoHome Parking. Continue on and there's an old road you can also use. Find somewhere safe to park, and move on if asked.

Spotting Hotel

Hotel Novotel Taipei Taoyuan Airport
1-1 Terminal South Road, Taoyuan County, Dayuan Township, 337 Taipei | +886 3398 0888 | www.novotel.com

The closest hotel to the airport, and situated between the two runways alongside the roads

REGULAR:
AirAsia
AirAsia X
AirBridgeCargo
Air Busan
Air Canada
Air China
Air France
Air Hong Kong
Air Japan
Air Macau
Air New Zealand
ANA Cargo
Asiana Airlines
Cargolux
Cathay Dragon
Cathay Pacific
Cebu Pacific
China Cargo Airlines
China Eastern
China Southern
Eastar Jet
Emirates
Far Eastern Air Transport
FedEx Express
Hainan Airlines
Hebei Airlines
Hong Kong Airlines
Japan Airlines
JC International
Jeju Air
Jetstar Asia
Jetstar Japan
Jetstar Pacific
Jin Air
Juneyao Airlines
KC International
KLM
Korean Air
Malaysia Airlines
Malindo Air
MASkargo
Nippon Cargo
NokScoot
Philippine Airlines
Philippines AirAsia
Polar Air Cargo

↓

which lead to the terminals. Even numbered rooms on floors 7, 8 and 9 face towards the runway 05L/R thresholds, and as such you can get views of many (but not all) movements depending on the direction in use.

Public Transport

Taoyuan is linked to the MRT metro system, as well as the bus network.

Scoot
SF Airlines
Shandong Airlines
Shenzhen Airlines
Sichuan Airlines
Singapore Airlines
Spring Airlines
StarFlyer
Thai Airways
Thai Lion Air
Turkish Airlines
T'way Air
United Airlines
UPS Airlines
Vanilla Air
Vietjet Air
Vietnam Airlines
XiamenAir
Yangtze River Express

OTHER AIRPORTS

Kaohsiung International

KHH | RCKH

A busy airport in the south of Taiwan. All of Taiwan's domestic airlines have a heavy presence here, including China Airlines, EVA Air, Far Eastern Air Transport, Uni Air and Tigerair Taiwan. International services include AirAsia X, Cathay Dragon, China Eastern, China Southern, Japan Airlines, Vietnam Airlines and XiamenAir. Over 6 million passengers used the airport in 2017.

Kaohsiung has a single runway and two terminals – domestic and international – both in the southwestern corner of the airport.

The best place to watch the action is in the covered walkway between the domestic and international terminals, were seating and large windows have views over many of the gates and ramp areas. This area is actually signposted the View Deck, so is easy to find (on the departures level).

Nearby is the Republic of China Air Force Museum (see later).

Taichung International

RMQ | RCMQ

One of Taiwan's newest airports, Taichung was opened in 2004 on a former air base in the west of the island. It has a north-south runway and two passenger terminals way off to the west of it. To its east are the still operational Ching Chuan Kang Air Force Base facilities.

The airport sees cross-straits flights to China by Air China, China Airlines, China Eastern, Mandarin Airlines, Tianjin Airlines and Uni Air, with others including EVA Air, HK Express, Tigerair Taiwan, T'way and Vietjet.

There are good views of the ramp within the terminal. Those with a car could use the car park of the Chingchuankang Golf Course near the threshold of runway 18 if aircraft are arriving from that direction, for good approach shots.

Former Republic of China Air Force Boeing 727 '2722' is preserved on the air base. It may be visible from departing aircraft.

MUSEUMS

Republic of China Air Force Museum

Jieshou West Road, Gangshan District, Kaohsiung City, Taiwan 820 | +886 7 625 8111

A smart military museum at the Gangshan Air Base north of Kaohsiung telling the story of Taiwan's air force. Also includes a Boeing 720, Douglas DC-3 and DC-6 and Curtiss C-46 among the 45 or so aircraft exhibits. Open Saturday and Sunday 9am-4.30pm.

THAILAND

Capital: Bangkok

Overview

Thailand is one of Asia's most visited countries with some major tourist attractions. As a result, it is a busy place for air travel, with carriers from all over the world to be found at the main airports. These can be found at Bangkok, which has two large airports, and the holiday island of Phuket. Many smaller airports have international flights, too.

Thai Airways is the modern national carrier, and Thailand is also home to a number of leisure and low-cost airlines. There are also a good number of preserved aircraft and museums around the country, many in unexpected roadside locations, or at airports and air bases.

Spotting is generally accepted and understood in Thailand, with facilities provided at some airports.

PRINCIPAL AIRPORTS

BANGKOK DON MUEANG

DMK | VTBD

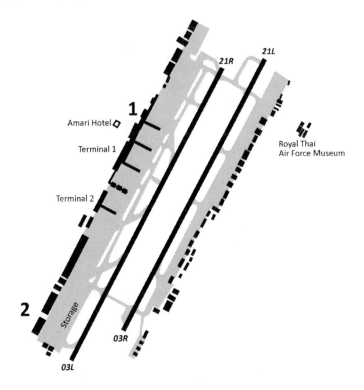

Originally Bangkok's main airport, Don Mueang closed when Suvarnabhumi opened in 2006, but has since grown again as a hub for low cost and domestic flights as a result of overcrowding at the new airport. The country's low-cost airlines are based here, and many other similar carriers fly in.

It now has two terminals – Terminal 1 for international flights, and Terminal 2 for domestic. There is a pair of parallel runways. Incredibly, there is a golf course wedged in between the two runways!

A number of airliners can be found stored to the south of the terminals, and there is a military

BASE FOR:
New Gen Airways
Nok Air
NokScoot
Orient Thai
Siam Air
Thai AirAsia
Thai AirAsia X
Thai Lion Air

↓

aviation museum to the east of the airfield (see later). Military movements, including the Royal Thai transport aircraft, add to the interest of visiting this airport. They operate from the base on the eastern side of the airport.

Spotting Locations

1. Terminal Viewing Area
The best place to spot is at the viewing terraces inside the terminal, split into north and south sections; each section is better depending on the direction of runway use. Photography is though glass, and recently signs indicated that this was not allowed; they have since been removed.

2. Storage Location
A number of stored aircraft are present at this airport. If you take bus 59 to the stop next to the Bangkok Airways hangar and then walk back to the terminal you will see many of these aircraft.

Spotting Hotels

Amari Hotel Don Mueang
333 Chert Wudthakas Road, Si Kan, Don Mueang, Bangkok 10210 | +66 2 566 1020 | www.amari.com/donmuang/

This hotel is connected to the terminals via a walkway. Rooms on floors 4 and above have views of aircraft once they have departed from runways 21L/R, or whilst on final approach. They cannot be seen on the ground.

Travel Between Bangkok Airports

A free shuttle bus links the two airports, operating from early morning till late at night. At Don Mueang the bus is on the ground floor at Terminal 1. At Suvarnabhumi the bus is level 2 between gates 2 and 3.

REGULAR:
AirAsia
China Express Airlines
Indonesia AirAsia
Indonesia AirAsia X
JC International
Malindo Air
Philippines AirAsia
Royal Thai Air Force
Tigerair Taiwan

BANGKOK SUVARNABHUMI

BKK | VTBS

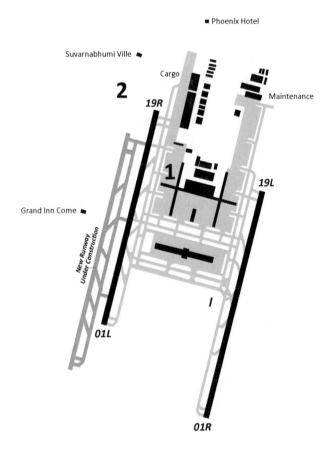

Suvarnabhumi Airport opened in 2006 as a replacement to the outdated and crowded Don Mueang Airport, which has since reopened. It is a sleek, modern facility with two runways, and is home to Thai Airways and any other airlines from the country. It is one of Asia's busiest airports, and the diversity of airlines both local and from around the world makes it a real draw for enthusiasts – especially with good spotting locations and hotels to use.

BASE FOR:
Asia Atlantic Airlines
Bangkok Airways
Jet Asia Airways
Thai Airways
Thai Smile
Thai VietJet Air

↓

The airport has a large terminal between the parallel runways, which spreads out in various directions. A new satellite terminal for domestic flights is expected to open in 2019, with another parallel runway also planned. With the airport already operating above capacity, it can't come soon enough.

Other areas of note at Suvarnabhumi include the maintenance base for Thai Airways, and a large freight facility, both north of the main terminal and visible from aircraft when arriving or departing.

Spotting Locations

1. Observation Area
Inside the terminal is an area set aside for watching aircraft, which is signposted. The views are good over the western side of the airport, and photography is possible with a long lens. Having nearby eateries and coffee shop also makes this a comfortable place to watch aircraft. You will not see the whole apron, but most movements will be visible at some point.

2. Western Perimeter
King Kaeo Road runs along the western side airfield, following alongside runway 1L/19R and the planned third runway site. It is possible to walk towards the airport from this road at various locations and take photos of arrivals or log what is visible parked at the passenger and cargo terminals. A long lens is needed. You will probably need to direct a taxi drive to reach the location.

3. Spotting Hotels
(see later).

REGULAR:
Aeroflot
Air Astana
Air Austral
Air China
Air France
Air Hong Kong
Air India
Air Italy
Air Macau
Air Mauritius
All Nippon Airways
Arkia
Asiana Airlines
Austrian Airlines
Azur Air
Beijing Capital
Biman Bangladesh
Bhutan Airlines
British Airways
Cardig Air
Cargolux
Cathay Pacific
Cebu Pacific
China Airlines
China Cargo Airlines
China Eastern
China Southern
Druk Air
Eastar Jet
EgyptAir
El Al
Emirates
Ethiopian Airlines
Etihad
Eurowings
EVA Air
FedEx Express
Finnair
Garuda Indonesia
Gulf Air
Hainan Airlines
Hebei Airlines
Hong Kong Airlines
IndiGo
Japan Airlines
JC International
Jeju Air
Jet Airways
Jetstar
Jin Air
Juneyao Airlines

↓

Spotting Hotels

Phoenix Hotel

88 Ladkrabang 7, Ladkrabang Road, Bangkok 10520
+66 2 737 1446 | www.phoenixhotelbangkok.com

The best-known hotel for spotting at
Suvarnabhumi airport. Management understand
the needs of spotters and will grant access to the
rooftop area and balcony facing final approach
to runway 19R. The hotel is only 2 miles from the
terminal and very affordable. Ask staff and they
can provide you with a list of the day's arrivals.

Grand Inn Come Hotel

99 Moo 6 Kingkaew Road, Rachathewa, Bangkok 10540
+66 2 738 8191 | www.grandinncome-hotel.com

A basic but pleasant hotel situated alongside the
airport perimeter to the west. Top floor rooms
overlook runway 19R/01L, with 541 reported as
having great views. Most movements can be seen
and tied up with SBS or flight tracker websites.
Photography is possible if you have a long lens
and can cope with the heat haze.

Suvarnabhumi Ville Bangkok

9/9 Moo 7 Soi Kingkaew 64, Kingkaew road, Rachathewa,
Bangkok 10540 | www.suvarnabhumiville.com

Another hotel close to the airport, with
comfortable rooms and decent prices. The top
floor of the block closest to the airport has a
small viewing platform on the roof which makes
a good location for photography (albeit backlit a
lot of the day). Many rooms also have balconies
with good views.

K-Mile Air
Kenya Airways
KLM
Korean Air
Kuwait Airways
Lanmei Airlines
Lao Airlines
Lucky Air
Lufthansa
Mahan Air
Malaysia Airlines
Maldivian
MIAT Mongolian
Myanmar Airways
International
Myanmar National
Nepal Airlines
Nippon Cargo
Nordwind Airlines
Norwegian
Okay Airways
Oman Air
Pakistan International
Peach
Philippine Airlines
Qantas
Qatar Airways
Regent Airways
Royal Brunei
Royal Jordanian
S7 Airlines
Scoot
Shandong Airlines
Shenzhen Airlines
Sichuan Airlines
Singapore Airlines
SpiceJet
Spring Airlines
SriLankans Airlines
Swiss International
Turkish Airlines
Turkmenistan Airlines
T'way Air
Ukraine International
UPS Airlines
Ural Airlines
US-Bangla Airlines
Uzbekistan Airways
Vietnam Airlines
XiamenAir
Yangtze River Express

PHUKET INTERNATIONAL

HKT | VTSP

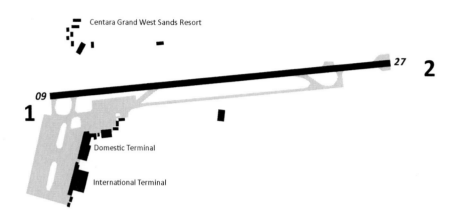

Phuket is one of Thailand's busiest airports thanks to the island's thriving holiday resorts. Traffic comes from Europe, the Middle East, Australia and the Far East, as well as from across Thailand. It is a mix of scheduled, low-cost and charters, with many wide body aircraft visiting. The busiest season is between November and March.

The airport spans a narrow point at the northern part of the island, with a single runway 09/27, and three terminals crowded round a parking apron at the western end. Nai Yang Beach and the Andaman Sea forms the western boundary.

A smoker's terrace airside in the international terminal has good views.

BASE FOR:
Bangkok Airways
Thai AirAsia
Thai Airways

↓

Spotting Locations

1. Nai Yang Beach
One of the most popular places to spot from is the beach separating the runway from the

sea. Photographers will love the proximity to aircraft landing and the stunning location. It is only really good if aircraft are landing on runway 09, however. To reach the beach, the nearest parking is along Soi Mai Khao 6, to the north of the airport. You'll then need to walk around half a mile along the path (or hire a scooter taxi).

2. Runway 27 Approach
The perimeter road running around the end of runway 27 is accessible, with a good viewpoint when this direction is in use. From the main Thepkasattri Rd which passes the eastern end of the airport, turn onto road 4031, then make a right along the track when the perimeter fence comes into view. Follow this to the end of the runway. Spotters often get moved on from here.

Spotting Hotels

Centara Grand West Sands Resort
Soi Mai Khao 4, Mai Khao, Thalang, Phuket 83110
+66 76 372 000 | www.centarahotelsresorts.com

A family resort hotel located close to Phuket Airport with great amenities and nearby beach. Some rooms have balconies and views of the airport apron and runway approach. Jonathan Payne, the Executive Assistant Manager, is keen to accommodate the needs of spotters. Call ahead to make a request for a room with the best views.

The Sixteenth – Naiyang Beach Resort
19/16, Mu1, Saku, Thalang, Phuket 83110
+66 76 530 187 8 | www.the16naiyanghotel.com

A new hotel a few minutes from the airport (with a free shuttle). Rooms are clean and air conditioned, and the hotel has a rooftop pool bar area which looks over the airport, with most parking stands visible. Single rooms face west towards the parking area, whilst twin rooms face east.

REGULAR:
Asiana Airlines
Azur Air
Beijing Capital
Cathay Dragon
China Eastern
China Southern
Chongqing Airlines
Edelweiss Air
Emirates
Etihad
Finnair
Firefly
Hainan Airlines
Hebei Airlines
HK Express
Jetstar Airways
Jetstar Asia
Jin Air
Juneyao Airlines
Korean Air
Kunming Airlines
Lucky Air
Malaysia Airlines
Malindo Air
Myanmar National
New Gen Airways
Nok Air
Nordwind Airlines
Okay Airways
Qatar Airways
Rossiya Airlines
Scoot
Shandong Airlines
Shenzhen Airlines
Sichuan Airlines
SilkAir
Spring Airlines
Thai Lion Air
Thai Smile
Thai VietJet Air
Tianjin Airlines
TUI Airways
Turkish Airlines
VietJet Air
XiamenAir

OTHER AIRPORTS

Chiang Mai International

CNX | VTCC

The busiest airport in northern Thailand, with a significant presence by Bangkok Airways and Thai AirAsia. Most flights are domestic, but international services are also operated by Asiana, Cathay Dragon, China Eastern, EVA Air, Hainan Airlines, Korean Air, Qatar Airways, Scoot, Sichuan Airlines and Spring Airlines among others. Flights to China are among the most common.

A Royal Thai Air Force Douglas DC-3 is based at the airport, usually parked near the end of runway 18.

The airport has a single north-south runway, with a passenger terminal on the eastern side. A footbridge crossing the main road running past the southern end of the airport is a great place to watch movements, and photograph arrivals on runway 36.

Chiang Rai International

CEI | VTCT

Located in northern Thailand, Chiang Rai handles domestic flights and some flights from China and Hong Kong. There are some views from the terminal, and those with a car can try the road which runs parallel to the runway on the eastern side. It has views through the fence.

Khon Kaen

KKC | VTUK

A small regional airport with links to Bangkok from the country's domestic and low cost carriers. There is a small terminal and just one runway, 03/21. Views are possible of the runway and apron from the car park next to the terminal.

Koh Samui

USM | VTSM

A fairly busy airport serving the island of the same name in the Gulf of Thailand. It has a single runway which aircraft must backtrack on due to the lack of parallel taxiway. Traffic is made up mainly leisure and low cost carriers flying to destinations in Thailand, Singapore, China and Malaysia.

There is a great spot just to the south of the terminal where you can park for free and get good views over the runway and terminal apron.

Krabi International

KBV | VTSG

Krabi is a relatively new airport, opened in 1999, and only a short distance from Phuket. It is a seasonal holiday destination with many long-haul charter flights from Europe. Other flights from across Asia sees airlines like China Eastern, Juneyao Airlines, Korean Air, Okay Airways, Scoot, and Sichuan Airlines complement the regular domestic carriers.

Two small terminals are soon to be joined by a third, larger terminal to help cope with demand at the airport.

Those with a car can find the perimeter road at the eastern end of the airport (for runway 32), where good views through the fence are possible. Head east along the main road from the terminals, then turn left onto road 4037. A small road turns left just after the runway end, leading to the spot.

U-Tapao International

UTP | VTBU

Situated between Rayong and Pattaya City to the south of Bangkok, U-Tapao International is an interesting airport.

As well as scheduled passenger services from airlines such as AirAsia, Bangkok Airways, China Southern, Donghai Airlines, Hainan Airlines, Kunming Airlines, Qatar Airways, Shenzhen Airlines and Thai Lion Air, it also sees seasonal charter flights from further afield.

The airport is also the main base of the Royal Thai Navy, whose aircraft are usually present.

On the eastern side of the airfield is a large Thai Airways maintenance facility. Many of the airline's older types have been stored here in recent years, with others coming and going for regular work.

Because of the military presence, spotting is difficult at U-Tapao, and photography is not advised. Passengers arriving and departing will be able to see aircraft on the ground, with distant views of stored aircraft.

A collection of preserved aircraft is on display inside the Navy base at the northern part of the airport. This is not usually open to the public, but access can be granted if you contact in advance. A Grumman Albatross is located at the base entrance.

Udon Thani International

UTH | VTUD

A primarily domestic airport, served by Nok Air, Thai AirAsia, Thai Lion Air and Thai Smile, with some cargo services. Udon Thani has a single runway and a terminal at the north-western end. The Royal Thai Air Force occupies a base at the southern end, with a Douglas DC-3 usually present. There are some views from around the terminal.

The Kavin Buri Green Hotel (299/99 Prajak Road, Makhaeng, Udon Thani 41000 | www.kavinburi.com) offers the best views of traffic. High floor rooms facing the airport have views of traffic approaching to just before touchdown, or just after departure. They have balconies. There is also a rooftop pool area with similar views.

MUSEUMS

Jesada Technik Museum
100 Moo 2 Ngewrai, 73120 Nakon Chaisri | +66 34 339 468

A large museum displaying all kinds of transportation, including historic cars and motorbikes. Aircraft in the collection include a Douglas DC-3 and NAMC YS-11. Located at Nakon Chaisri in the western suburbs of Bangkok. Open daily except Monday, 9am-5pm.

Royal Thai Air Force Museum
Don Mueang Airport, Bangkok 10210 | +66 2 534 1853
www.rtaf.mi.th/Pages/Tourist_Attractions.aspx

A collection of retired aircraft that have a connection with the Royal Thai Air Force, located next to Don Mueang Airport. Includes everything from early prop types through fighter jets, helicopters and even a Boeing 737-200. Open daily except Monday, 8am-3.30pm.

VIETNAM

Capital: Hanoi

Overview

Vietnam is growing in stature as a centre for aviation thanks to the successful growth of Vietnam Airlines and the tourism industry here. The two main airports are at Hanoi and Ho Chi Minh City, at either end of the country, with Da Nang in the centre also of interest.

The country is easy to get to, and welcoming to visitors, but be careful when using binoculars and cameras around airports as the hobby can be misunderstood in this Communist country.

For those intent on exploring, various retired airliners from days gone by can be found, particularly in Hanoi and Ho Chi Minh City (see our book Preserved Airliners of Asia & Australasia for more details).

PRINCIPAL AIRPORTS

HANOI NOI BAI INTERNATIONAL

HAN | VVNB

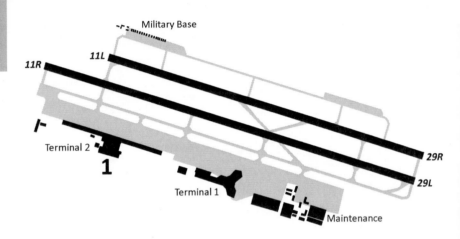

Military Base

11L

11R

Terminal 2

1

29R

29L

Terminal 1

Maintenance

Vietnam's second major gateway, after Ho Chi Minh City, is located in the north of the country and acts as a hub for international traffic and regional flights, with many long-haul links and connections around Asia.

The airport is to the north of the city, across the Red River. It has two parallel runways, with the two terminals, cargo terminal, and Vietnam Airlines engineering facility strung out along the southern side. The modern international Terminal 2 was opened in 2014 to cater for growing demand at the airport.

On the northern side is a small military base where fighter jets are housed under shelters. There are views airside in both terminals, with those in Terminal 1 being better.

BASE FOR:
Cambodia Angkor Air
Jetstar Pacific
VietJet Air
Vietnam Airlines

↓

Spotting Location

1. Terminal 2

Landside in the terminal you'll find a food court with seating and views over the nearby gates and the runway. You can also see the military area in the distance. The domestic terminal is not visible from here. The glass is clean and good for taking pictures through, but the area can get crowded at times.

Spotting Hotel

Anova Hotel

Vo Nguyen Giap Street, Thai Phu, Mai Dinh Commune, Soc Son District, Ha Noi | www.anovahotel.com

One of the nearest good quality hotels to the airport, situated just over a mile from the domestic terminal. Some rooms have views of aircraft on approach or after departure. You will need flight trackers to tie up movements, and photographs can be difficult due to the distance and tinted glass.

REGULAR:
Aeroflot
AirAsia
Air China
Air France Cargo
Air Macau
All Nippon Airways
Asiana Airlines
Bangkok Airways
Cardig Air
Cathay Dragon
Cathay Pacific Cargo
Cebu Pacific
China Airlines
China Eastern
China Southern
Chongqing Airlines
Eastar Jet
Emirates
Etihad Cargo
EVA Air
FedEx Express
Hainan Airlines
Hong Kong Airlines
Japan Airlines
Jeju Air
Jin Air
Korean Air
K-Mile Air
Lanmei Airlines
Lao Airlines
Lucky Air
Malaysia Airlines
Malindo Air
Mandarin Airlines
Qatar Airways
Scoot
Silk Air
Singapore Airlines
Thai AirAsia
Thai Airways
Thai Lion Air
Turkish Airlines
VASCO

HO CHI MINH CITY
TAN SON NHAT INTERNATIONAL

SGN | VVTS

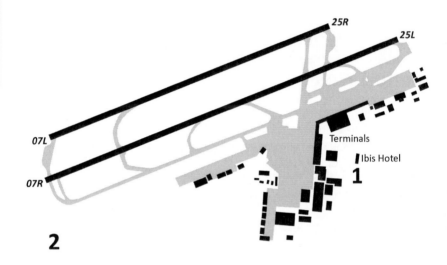

Tan Son Nhat International is Vietnam's busiest airport and the main home base of Vietnam Airlines and other carriers. Despite adding a modern international terminal in 2007, the airport is overcrowded and in need of further expansion and upgrade.

Alongside the international terminal is a domestic terminal, a busy cargo hub, and areas of parking for local and executive aircraft. The airport has a pair of parallel runways.

Spotting is difficult at this airport, however the Ibis hotel is perfect for some privacy and relaxation. The terminal buildings have plenty of views, and there are some views when approaching the airport by road.

BASE FOR:
Jetstar Pacific
VASCO
VietJet Air
Vietnam Airlines

↓

Spotting Locations

1. Ibis Hotel

An easier way to spot at Ho Chi Minh city than by tackling the roads (see later).

2. Cong Hoa

This street is to the west of the terminal area and passes close to the end of the runway. A café on the high floors of 602 Cong Hoa has an outdoor terrace and good views of aircraft on approach if coming from the west.

Spotting Hotels

Ibis Ho Chi Minh City Airport

2 Hong Ha Street, Ho Chi Minh, Ho Chi Minh City 700000
+84 8 3848 5556 | www.ibis.com

A fairly new hotel. King rooms on floors 7 and up in the *18-*26 range have views of aircraft landing and departing, but not on the ground as the airport terminal is in the way. There is also a rooftop pool bar area. A strong camera lens will give you some good shots.

REGULAR:
Aeroflot
Air Astana
Air China
Air France
Air Hong Kong
AirAsia
All Nippon Airways
Asiana Airlines
Cambodia Angkor Air
Cargolux
Cathay Pacific
Cebu Pacific
China Airlines
China Eastern
China Southern
Chongqing Airlines
Emirates
EVA Air
FedEx Express
Hong Kong Airlines
Japan Airlines
Jeju Air
Jetstar Airways
Korean Air
Lanmei Airlines
Lao Airlines
Malaysia Airlines
Malindo Air
Mandarin Airlines
Nok Air
Philippine Airlines
Philippines AirAsia
Qatar Airways
Raya Airways
Royal Brunei
Scoot
Sichuan Airlines
Singapore Airlines
Spring Airlines
Thai AirAsia
Thai Airways
Thai Lion Air
Turkish Airlines
T'way Airlines
XiamenAir

OTHER AIRPORTS

Cam Ranh International

CXR | VVCR

Only opened to passenger traffic in 2004, this former military base now handles almost 5 million passengers per year. Most flights are domestic, or to Chinese destinations. Airlines like AirAsia, Bangkok Airways, Jetstar Pacific, VietJet Air and Vietnam Airlines make up the bulk of flights, but you'll also see Chinese carriers, and regular charters from Russian airlines during peak season.

The terminal is small, with some views both from inside and the car park outside of aircraft parked on the apron.

Da Nang International

DAD | VVDN

Da Nang is Vietnam's third-busiest airport, located on the coast in the centre of the country. It handles flights from across Asia, primarily from Jetstar Pacific and Vietnam Airlines. Others of interest include Air Seoul, Asiana, Beijing Capital, Cathay Dragon, China Southern, Eastar Jet, Jeju Air, Jin Air, Korean air, Sichuan Airlines, SilkAir and T'way Airlines. Da Nang has seen massive growth, from handling 1 million passengers per annum in 2006 to 11 million in 2017.

The airport has two runways, with both international and domestic terminals on the eastern side and a long parking apron stretching north to south.

On the western side of the airport as well as to the south of the terminal is the military Da Nang Air Base. These areas should be avoided.

There are views inside the terminals once airside. You may also want to head to Le Daj Hanh, a road which passes the southern end of the airport and has plenty of cafés and locations to watch arrivals from the south.

Phu Quoc International

PQC | VVPQ

A new airport in Phu Quoc island, which opened to traffic in 2012 and has an ambitious expansion plan as growth continues. It is served by AirAsia, Bangkok Airways, China Southern, Donghai Airlines, Jetstar Pacific, Lucky Air, VietJet Air and Vietnam Airlines. It also handles long-haul charters from Europe and Russia.

There are views airside within the terminal, and also some views of the parking apron and runway if you walk to the west outside the terminal entrance.

MUSEUMS

Vietnam Military History Museum
28A Điên Biên Phú, Điên Biên, Ba Đình, Hà Nôi | www.btlsqsvn.org.vn
Located in central Hanoi, near the Imperial Citadel. Among its interesting exhibits are various military aircraft including an Ilyushin Il-14. Open Tue, Wed, Thu, Sat, Sun, 8am-11am and 1pm-4.30pm.

OTHER BOOKS FOR AVIATION ENTHUSIASTS

Airport Spotting Guides UK & Ireland

Airport Spotting Guides USA

World Airports Spotting Guides

Lost Airline Colours of Europe

Preserved Airliners of North America

Preserved Airliners of Asia & Australasia

Preserved Airliners of Europe